Memory Activities for Language Learning

Cambridge Handbooks for Language Teachers

This series, now with over 40 titles, offers practical ideas, techniques and activities for the teaching of English and other languages providing inspiration for both teachers and trainers.

Recent titles in this series:

Memory Activities for Language Learning

Nick Bilbrough

Consultant and editor: Scott Thornbury

CAMBRIDGE
UNIVERSITY PRESS

CAMBRIDGE
UNIVERSITY PRESS

University Printing House, Cambridge CB2 8BS, United Kingdom

One Liberty Plaza, 20th Floor, New York, NY 10006, USA

477 Williamstown Road, Port Melbourne, VIC 3207, Australia

4843/24, 2nd Floor, Ansari Road, Daryaganj, Delhi – 110002, India

79 Anson Road, #06–04/06, Singapore 079906

Cambridge University Press is part of the University of Cambridge.

It furthers the University's mission by disseminating knowledge in the pursuit of
education, learning and research at the highest international levels of excellence.

www.cambridge.org
Information on this title: www.cambridge.org/9780521132411

First published 2011
20 19 18 17 16 15 14 13 12 11 10 9 8 7 6 5 4 3

Printed in Great Britain by CPI Group (UK) Ltd, Croydon CR0 4YY

A catalogue record for this publication is available from the British Library

Library of Congress Cataloguing in Publication data
Bilbrough, Nick.
  Memory activities for language learning / Nick Bilbrough.
    p. cm.
  Includes bibliographical references and index.
  ISBN 978-0-521-13241-1 (pbk. with cd rom)
1. Language and languages – Study and teaching. 2. Memory. I. Thornbury, Scott,
  1950– II. Title.
  P53.B53 2011
  418.0071–dc22

                                                  2010050056

ISBN 978-0-521-13241-1 Paperback and CD-ROM

Contents

Thanks and acknowledgements

Many thanks to Scott Thornbury for making it happen and for unfailing support throughout, and to Jacque French and Ruth Atkinson for enthusiastic, eagle-eyed editorial guidance.

For trialling ideas and allowing me to use examples of their work, thanks too to students and teachers at Horizon Language Training and Totnes School of English (Totnes), Brasshouse Language Centre (Birmingham), SOAS (London), Instituto Federal Sul-Rio-Grandense (Charqueadas) and Escola de Formação de Professores Garcia Neto (Luanda).

I am indebted to Symon Rawles and Anna Rawles, Ed Francis and Louise Francis, Jon Bilbrough, Helen Thompson, Silvia Sisitkova, Eva Salo, Annika Ruohonen and Kate Rudman for allowing me to raid their photo collections; to Raffaele Maria Sciarra, Manuela Huber, Gudrun Bayeride and Rieko Shoon for providing drawings; and to Chia Suan Chong, Emma Lay, Camille Chardon, Vera Sevastyanova, Conrado Abreu Chagas and Régis for examples of writing.

Special thanks to Francisco Matete, Michalis Sivvas, Angelica Fernando and Suzie Bewell's Year 10 French class at All Saints RC School, York, for sharing insights into their own language learning strategies, to Anil Biltoo for speedily finding a Pali meal chant and to James Risebero for supplying a drawing of a carnivorous radiator at very short notice.

Text

copyright © Julia Donaldson 2007. Illustration copyright © Axel Scheffler 2007. Reproduced with the permission of Alison Green Books an imprint of Scholastic Ltd. All Rights Reserved; Cambridge University Press for the text on p. 115 from *English in Mind Student's Book 1*, Second edition, by Herbert Puchta and Jeff Stranks. Copyright © Cambridge University Press 2010. Reproduced with permission; Dr Valerie J. Roebuck for advice on the Pali chant on pp. 163–4; David Lynch for the text on p. 169 taken from *Mulholland Drive*. Reproduced with permission.

Photos

The publishers are grateful to the following for permission to reproduce photographic material inside the textbook:

p. 57 Box 2.7: © Superstock/Superstock; p. 121 Box 4.10: Nick Bilbrough; p. 126 Box 4.13a: Helen Thompson; p. 126 Box 4.13b: Symon Rawles; p. 156 Helen Thompson; p. 167 Box 6.1: Topfoto/The Granger Collection, New York.

The publishers are grateful to the following for permission to reproduce photographic material on the CD-ROM:

Box 4.13a – photo 1: Kate Rudman; photo 2: © David White/Alamy; photos 3 and 5: Jon Bilbrough; photo 4: Annika Ruohonen; photo 6: Helen Thompson; photo 7: Anna Rawles; photo 8: © Lourens Smak/Alamy; Box 4.13b – photo 1: Louise Francis; photo 2: © Aflo Co. Ltd/Alamy; photo 3: Ed Francis; photo 4: © Oliver Knight/Alamy; photo 5: Eva Salo; photo 6: Louise Francis; photo 7: Symon Rawles; photo 8: Jon Bilbrough.

Commissioned artwork

For the artwork on p. 55 Box 2.6: Manuela Huber; p. 84 Box 3.2b: Raffaele Maria Sciarra, Manuela Huber, Gudrun Bayeride, Rieko Shoon; p. 144 Box 5.5a: James Risebero. Additional artwork: Servis Filmsetting Ltd. Stockport, Cheshire.

Introduction

Why this book?

There is no learning without remembering. And language learning – perhaps more than most other forms of learning – places huge demands on memory. As language teachers, whatever our teaching context, or the age, goals or learning style of our learners, or the materials we use or the methods we favour, in the end our aim is to optimize our learners' memory for language – to help them remember the sounds, words, chunks, structures and textual conventions of the target language. Whether we do this through an explicit focus on form, through rich and varied exposure, through plentiful opportunities to use the language in meaningful ways, or through a combination of all three, the cognitive processes of memory are central to everything we do.

We may be the most dedicated professionals, working in well-equipped classrooms, setting up enjoyable activities for highly motivated learners, but without also engaging the memory skills of the people we work with – their abilities to recognize, to notice, to process, to store, to retrieve and to reactivate language – very little can be achieved.

So if we want language to be remembered, and if we want our learners to become more proficient in remembering – both in class and independently – we need a bank of activities that can facilitate these processes. It is with this purpose in mind that this book has been written.

The role of memory in language learning

Memory underpins every aspect of successful language learning. It is the glue that binds us to the world of language around us and within us. As consumers and producers of language, we depend on our memories both to interpret spoken and written texts, and to speak and write effectively. Without memory, we also have no means of developing in these skills.

Most linguists would endorse this: Skehan (1998), for instance, maintains that having a good memory is a key component of language aptitude (the other components being auditory ability and pattern recognition). In many parts of the world, there has always been a strong focus on memory in educational settings, and the memorization of word lists, dialogues and even entire texts has remained a very popular tool for the language classroom. But memorizing as a language-learning activity has not always been viewed favourably by language-teaching methodologists and materials writers. This scepticism can be at least partially traced to Noam Chomsky's (1959) critique of behaviourism, and his emphasis on the creative nature of language. If, as he claimed, much of what we write and say is totally unique in form, what purpose might there be in memorizing the borrowed words of others?

Thus, from the 1960s onwards, in North America and Western Europe in particular, the discrediting of behaviourist theory as an effective language-teaching methodology led to the widely shared view that memorization was a dry and meaningless activity, in conflict with a learner's natural ability to create unique and original utterances. And since then the debate has raged. Is language production an entirely creative process, or do we also depend on a bank of pre-fabricated language items stored in our mental lexicons?

Dwight Bolinger, among others, has argued that the role of memory in retrieving stored language items from long-term memory is as important – if not more so – than being able to piece these items together to make coherent utterances: 'Speakers do as much remembering as they do putting together' (Bolinger, 1961). Or as another linguist has put it: 'Language is ... to be viewed as a kind of pastiche, pasted together in an improvised way out of ready-made elements' (Hopper, 1998).

More recently, the work of Michael Lewis and Dave Willis in particular (who were in turn influenced by the findings of corpus linguistics) has been representative of the increased interest in the viewpoint that language is 'grammaticised lexis' (Lewis, 1993). According to this view, fluency in a language is the result of having a stored bank (or 'phrasicon') of memorized chunks. This allows the speaker to assemble utterances in real time, without the need to generate each utterance from scratch, using an internalized grammar. Perhaps, as Lewis (1997) observes, 'we are much less original in using language than we like to believe'.

Wray (2008) has coined the term Morpheme Equivalent Unit (MEU) to refer to a word string or chunk of language that is processed like a morpheme, i.e. without the need to process the meaning of its component parts. So an expression like *at the end of the day* can be both stored and reproduced without any explicit focus on the individual words that it contains.

Other scholars, including Nick Ellis, have argued that these formulaic chunks may contain the 'seeds' of subsequent grammatical knowledge. In other words, these chunks 'release' their grammar over time. In practical terms, this means, for instance, that a learner can develop an understanding of how the present perfect is used by first noticing, and subsequently memorizing, some chunks of language in which it occurs. This is contrary to the widely held belief that a structure must first be learnt before it can be used to generate utterances by slotting in appropriate vocabulary items.

If it is not only individual words and grammar that need to be remembered, but also the vast number of chunks that are required for fluent communication, then the demands on our memories are far greater than was previously thought. If all of these items are to be stored successfully, then a focus on both making language as memorable as possible and using explicit memorization activities would seem to make sense.

Memory and texts

Memory also plays three key roles in the interpretation of spoken and written texts. First, there is the need to be able to retrieve the meanings of the individual words and chunks that make up the text. Some researchers, such as Paul Nation, have estimated that we need to understand at least 95% of the words in a text in order to be able to predict accurately the meaning of the remaining 5%. Except when processing the most simple texts, this 95% 'tipping point' represents a large passive vocabulary – of at least 3,000 items, by some calculations, and possibly a lot more. In some skills-based approaches to reading and listening – which have instead emphasized the top-down skills of predicting, guessing from context, and skimming and scanning, for example – the need to have a critical mass of word knowledge to enable understanding has been somewhat undervalued.

Secondly, there is the role of working memory in processing each new element that we read or listen to, and in linking these to the elements that have already been interpreted. Research has shown that fast, proficient readers tend to have high working-memory spans, and because of this they are able to focus simultaneously on a higher number of complex and sometimes unrelated ideas. Thirdly, without long-term memory – in the form of mental representations of how texts are organized, as well as our knowledge of the world – we would not be able to bring our experience to bear in making sense of texts at all.

Similarly, when we speak or write, memory allows us to retrieve words, chunks and grammatical forms from our mental lexicons for active use as they are required. The more effectively we do this, the more able we are to produce language that communicates our intended messages smoothly and concisely, and the more effectively we can organize texts in ways that make them intelligible to others. In writing this paragraph, I am aware that I am going through a process of scanning my own mental lexicon for appropriate language items to use, evaluating each option in working memory as it is retrieved, and discarding words that fail to express my intended meaning.

A good memory also enables us to produce text that is cohesive. Through my ability to retain the content of previously mentioned ideas in my working memory, I am able to provide links back to them with discourse markers and back referencing (such as the use of *also* near the beginning of the last sentence). And because I can also hold on to the form of what I have said, I am able to avoid the overuse of particular words.

Lastly, memory contributes to the overall coherence of a text by enabling its author to keep the purpose and the audience of the communication constantly in mind. I hope that mine is not letting me down too much here!

How does a memory for language work?

With memory being such a key skill in language learning (some have suggested that it is the fifth skill, alongside listening, speaking, reading and writing), it is surprising that comparatively little has been written about how the processes involved in remembering items in a second language may work. One explanation for this is that, as with much research into the brain's functions, little can be deduced with absolute certainty.

Below is a list of commonly used terms relating to memory that may be involved in the remembering of language. Though most writers about memory mention these terms, not everyone agrees on exactly how these different elements interact in the storage of new language.

- *Working memory*: Our senses are the first port of call for everything that we pay attention to around us. Working memory allows us to hold on to this data for a brief period of time so that we are able to manipulate it and process it consciously. So is this merely a more modern term for what was traditionally known as short-term memory? Not exactly. The concept of working memory, unlike that of short-term memory, implies a *state* in which things happen, rather than being merely a *place* through which language passes. It is limited not only by time, but also by capacity: only a small amount of data (five to nine pieces of information) can be maintained and processed in working memory at any given time. For more on the components that make up working memory, see the introduction to Chapter 1.

- *Long-term memory*: The storage of information in long-term memory – unlike in working memory – is a largely subconscious process and is apparently not constrained by either time or capacity. Material can be stored in long-term memory for anything between a few days and a lifetime, depending on the richness of links that were made with existing material in the initial encoding, and on the regularity of opportunities to retrieve and reactivate it. For more on what factors may help with the storage of information in long-term memory, see the introduction to Chapter 2.
- *Declarative memory*: Everything in long-term memory that we are able to access consciously can be referred to as *declarative memory*. This, in turn, may be broken down into *semantic memory* – knowledge about the meaning of a word, facts and figures about the world, etc. – and *episodic memory* – personal memories that relate to past events in our lives. Language classes all over the world focus extensively on remembering information about the language being learnt, and this data may be stored as declarative memories. For instance, learners may be taught and may remember that the past tense of *go* is *went*, that prepositions are followed by *-ing* forms of verbs, or that the English for the Arabic لا شكر على واجب is 'don't mention it'. Of course, being able to retrieve this information when asked does not necessarily mean that the learners will be able to use these same areas of language when required to in spontaneous communication.
- *Procedural memory*: Long-term memory also includes some memories that may be difficult, or even impossible, to consciously access. Their existence is nevertheless evident in our ability to perform certain tasks, such as tying our shoelaces, swimming or driving. No attention is generally necessary in order to access our memory of how to do these things, and if we consciously try to retrieve exactly what is happening, we may even struggle to do so. I recently tried to explain to my 14-year-old son how to make bread using the bread machine in our house, something that I do nearly every day of my life, but I found I was able to recall exact quantities only by actually putting the ingredients into the machine myself, and forcing myself to focus on what I was doing. In language-learning terms, there are links here with the concept of *automaticity* and *flow*. The more fluent we are as speakers, the more able we are to produce language with limited or no effort on the part of working memory at all. That is, we can express ourselves effectively without paying much conscious attention to what we are saying.

A model of memory

There are essentially three processes involved in remembering language: *encoding*, *storage* and *retrieval*. *Encoding* is how we make sense of data that we hear or read by linking it to existing knowledge; *storage* is putting this data into long-term memory; and *retrieval* refers to the way in which data is brought back from memory in order to be used.

Of the vast amount of spoken and written language that we are exposed to through our senses, we pay attention to only a small proportion, and a part of this enters our working memories. Only a very limited amount of what has entered working memory will in turn get stored in long-term memory and eventually be available for meaningful output in speech or writing.

So how may this relate to what happens in the language classroom? As teachers we provide plenty of input to the learners, in the form of reading and listening material, explanations about language, and writing on the board; we maximize the potential for processing this exposure in working memory by setting up activities like drills, gap-fills and other practice activities; and when the learner speaks or writes in freer activities, the teacher can see how much language has actually been retained in long-term memory and can provide further input to address any gaps.

But there is more to remembering language than pouring water from a jug into a series of empty and leaky vessels, and hoping that some of it will stay there! Knowledge is not just a commodity that is passed from one place to another without any form of interaction with the existing contents. Learners also bring a vast amount of prior knowledge and experience to the proceedings and use this in creative ways in the storage of new language.

Most memory researchers now acknowledge that what is already stored in long-term memory actually plays a huge part in the acquisition of new data, and that there is a two-way process of interaction between working memory and long-term memory that is essential both in storage and in working-memory processing. This can be seen in the following diagram adapted from Earl Stevick, *Memory, Meaning and Method*, Second edition (Boston: Heinle and Heinle, 1996).

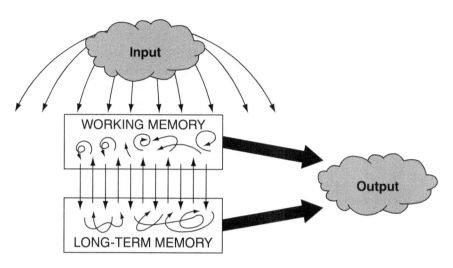

When new language data enters working memory, it immediately activates areas of existing knowledge in long-term memory and searches for links between them. Bryant (1990) has suggested that items in long-term memory are stored in 'dynamic networks' in which activation of one area leads to subconscious and rapid connections throughout the whole of long-term memory, which in turn can relay back new information to be processed in working memory. There may also be significant interaction between working memory and long-term memory in language production. When we speak fluently, we may be drawing directly from long-term memory, but when talking in a second language, there will often also be substantial working-memory involvement as we consciously plan, evaluate alternatives and restructure what is to be said.

Storing language in long-term memory, then, involves some complex and multifaceted interaction between working memory and long-term memory. It depends upon an ability to link new information with existing knowledge and to reflect upon these links. As already discussed, many linguists are now less inclined to regard the production of language as an entirely creative activity, recognizing that we rely to a greater extent than formerly believed on the retrieval and recycling of previously stored chunks and formulaic language. But learning a language, like teaching a language, is unquestionably still a creative process. Perhaps the element of creativity, however, lies as much in the process by which we store new language in long-term memory as in that of activating language from it.

What makes material memorable?

This link between creativity and memory can also play its part in the choice of materials that teachers and materials designers present to learners. In my twenty years as a language teacher, I have used a wide range of different teaching materials in many diverse contexts. One coursebook activity that sticks out in my mind as being particularly memorable is the reading maze in *Language in Use: Intermediate, Student's Book 1* by A. Doff and C. Jones (Cambridge University Press, 1994), which includes the short text below.

> A year ago, you were driving your cab when you saw a couple fighting in the street. The woman shouted 'He's going to kill me!' and jumped into your cab. She turned out to be a Hollywood movie star – she gave you a large tip and asked for your address. Last month she died, leaving you £500,000 in her will, 'To the taxi driver who saved my life'. Add that to your savings, plus £10,000 from driving your taxi.
>
> A friend back home is starting a business designing children's toys and has invited you to join her – it might be a good way to invest all that money. Or you could celebrate by going on a trip around the world …
>
> | Go into the toy business | ➤ | **3** | (p. 23) |
> | Go round the world | ➤ | **17** | (p. 115) |

In this activity, learners read a series of scenarios like this, and after each one, they have to make a decision, in pairs, about how to proceed. When they have agreed, they then go on to read the next text that they have chosen. Their objective is to make as much money as possible. It is an activity that my learners have enjoyed immensely and that I have always got a lot out of too; it has invariably promoted some motivated reading and processing of the text, as well as a lot of animated discussion.

If an activity like this is memorable for those who engage with it, then the time spent processing it may be increased and enriched, and consequently the potential for learning from it also improves. For educational psychologists Chip Heath and Dan Heath (2008), this 'memorability factor' is the key issue to address in deciding on the format in which to present material to be learnt. They have spent a great deal of their professional lives researching this area and have identified six criteria to facilitate the process of making material memorable. These are *simplicity, unexpectedness, concreteness, credibility, emotions* and *stories*, the first letter of which form the easily remembered acronym SUCCES. These criteria may be outlined as follows:

- *Simplicity*: It is difficult to remember anything that is too complex to understand or that is cloaked in too much unnecessary waffle. In the reading maze, the text is written at a level that is accessible for an intermediate-level learner, while not being so simple that there is no challenge in terms of new vocabulary. The reader is given just enough information to enable them to understand what the situation is, and to be able to make an informed decision, based on what has been read.
- *Unexpectedness*: People are more likely to pay attention to something, and consequently remember it, if it goes against what is expected. Reading a text about yourself, in which you are the one who is making the decisions, is quite a novel way of doing things and will be a new experience for most people. The maze also arouses curiosity about what will happen next, which is a great way of maintaining interest and motivating the reader to carry on.
- *Concreteness*: Visualization is central to the storage of new information in long-term memory, but it is far more difficult to visualize abstract material than that which is clear and concrete. The maze describes events that have happened, that are happening and that are going to a happen, in a way that faciliates the creation of such images by the reader.
- *Credibility*: We quickly lose interest in ideas that are outlandish and unbelievable. In the reading maze, a number of exciting and dramatic events unfold, but still the maze is rooted in the day-to-day struggles of human existence. The challenge to make the right decisions in life in order to be successful is something that most people can identify with very strongly.
- *Emotions*: There is a powerful link between emotion and memory. Advertisers around the world have made extensive use of this fact by creating adverts that deliberately amuse, arouse or even annoy us. The reading maze is something of an emotional rollercoaster, involving dramatic themes such as reward, bankruptcy, fame and kidnapping. The fact that these events are happening to the reader, rather than to a third party, makes the degree of emotional involvement even more powerful.

- *Stories*: We remember the information contained in a story far more easily than if it were presented as a list of facts. Just think how many stories, in some format or other, we tell and listen to during the course of a day. The stories we hear often serve as a sort of mental rehearsal for our own lives, so it is as if we are programmed to hold on to things that come to us in this way. A very strong narrative element runs through the entire maze, and this helps us to immerse ourselves in the events and retain information almost without effort.

As language teachers, these are important issues to consider when deciding on the kinds of material we present to our learners, and on the types of activities to adopt. But memory is also a factor to consider when reflecting on our everyday classroom routines.

Incorporating memory activities into classroom routines

Building a focus on memory into the regular routines of the classroom is another way of increasing memorability. Not only can it help learners appreciate exactly what they are learning and provide a strong sense of achievement, but it may also raise awareness about what has not been remembered and may therefore require further work. Here are some ways of incorporating memory activities into a range of situations that commonly occur in the language classroom.

Presenting language

The board, be it black, white or interactive, is still the most widely used resource available to teachers. It is a fantastic way of drawing learners' attention to an area of language and helping everyone to focus simultaneously on forms and meanings. When teachers use it to present language, often the learners immediately copy down what is written into their notebooks. However, if we want learners to focus, and consequently to build stronger memory traces, discouraging copying during presentations (which can be distracting) and instead allowing time for the learners to copy afterwards may be more beneficial. In this way, and provided the presentation itself is made memorable by, for example, the use of graphics, images, humour and drama, there is a greater chance that the learners will remember the useful information about the language that the teacher is sharing.

Traditionally, language-presentation stages may include a focus on meaning, spelling, pronunciation, context and collocations. A focus on mnemonics – a kind of 'trick' to help make the language more memorable – is also something worth including, where appropriate. This could involve linking a new word to other words that sound similar, using an acronym to help remember the various parts of a sentence, or building the language into a chant. See Chapter 5 for more details and further ideas.

Language on the board

By the end of a class, a teacher's board may be filled with the language that has been focused on during the course of the lesson. It could contain individual words (sometimes showing phonemic transcripts or stress patterns), chunks and expressions, or example sentences to illustrate a particular area of grammar. Some teachers' board work is highly planned and organized, while others use the board as a sort of notepad, writing up language items randomly as they come up in class. Either way, this is a very useful resource that can be exploited when incorporating memory activities.

If working with an interactive whiteboard, there is, of course, the option of saving the entire screen so that the language can easily be returned to in another class, or used to plan retrieval exercises. Some teachers without interactive whiteboards take a photo of the board at the end of each lesson with the same purpose in mind.

It is also worth spending a few minutes at the end of class just trying to get learners to retrieve the language that is on the board. One way of doing this is for learners to position themselves in pairs or small groups so that only one person can see it. The people who cannot see have to try and recall, aloud, what is written there. The person who can see the board tells them if they are right and supplies prompts, in the form of definitions, descriptions or mimes, where necessary.

Prompts can also be used by the teacher as a way to retrieve the board work. The teacher rubs out everything but the first letter of each word. Learners then work in pairs and try to recall everything that was written there, using the first letters as a memory trigger.

Another way of doing this is with the whole class working together. Everyone has a chance to try to remember what is written on the board before it is cleaned completely. As a group they then have to rewrite everything that was there, as accurately and as quickly as possible. Several people can write, or one person can be appointed as the scribe while the others call things out. If the teacher can remember anything that the class did not, the teacher wins – otherwise the class wins.

Gap-fill exercises

The gap-fill exercises typically found in coursebooks, where learners need to write in a missing word, are a good way to check the class's ability to use a particular area of language. When working with large, mixed-ability classes, however, the time needed to complete such an exercise will often vary immensely between different learners. What can the teacher do in this situation? If you stop the activity when the quicker learners have finished, the others will be deprived of the learning opportunity that the activity provides. On the other hand, if you wait until everyone has completed the exercise, how do you stop the fast finishers getting bored? One solution is to provide an extra memory challenge for those who have finished. Learners can be asked to try to remember as many of the sentences as possible before testing each other in pairs. Alternatively, one learner can read out the sentence, saying 'buzz' where the gaps are, and the other learner has to supply the missing word.

Reading and listening material

When I first trained to be a teacher, one of the things that was impressed on me during the course was the importance of incorporating pair work as soon as possible after the learners had engaged with a reading and listening text, and definitely before learners could be expected to provide feedback on what they had understood to the rest of the class. This advice is something that has stood the test of time for me and is still generally part of the way I teach today. Not only does it allow learners to build confidence before having to speak in front of a large group, but it also provides the opportunity for immediate activation of some of the language contained in the text, before it is lost from working memory. If we want learners to retain the items of language in a reading and listening text, then encouraging them to process it as much as possible, ideally through speech, can help to achieve this. One of the most effective tasks to accompany any kind of text is simply to ask learners to discuss in pairs everything they can remember about it.

This reactivation of language also applies to the extensive reading and listening that learners may do outside the class, of course. Allocating learners some class time for discussing the material they are accessing in their own time can help to facilitate this.

Speaking and writing activities

Many teachers now adopt a process approach to developing writing skills where learners are encouraged to plan, draft, edit and redraft their work.

Not only does this invariably lead to a more polished finished product, it also leads to more processing of the language the learners are using in their texts, and consequently to more remembering.

Building in an extra stage to a speaking activity where learners recall and reflect on what was said is another way of encouraging deeper processing of language and raising self-awareness about the learners' strengths and weaknesses. At the end of a mingling activity, for instance where learners walk around class interviewing different people, it may be useful to ask everyone to talk to the person next to them about who they spoke to and what was said. When learners are engaged in a speaking activity in small groups, it is often useful to incorporate a stage at the end where a spokesperson from each group reports back to the whole class on what they have been discussing. Not only does this let other groups know what they have been doing and promote some recycling of the language they have used, but it can also encourage a greater focus on accuracy and improve performance levels.

Another way of doing this is to appoint a 'listener' in each group. This person's task is to listen to the conversation without taking an active role. At various points in the discussion, the listener intervenes and summarizes, by giving feedback on who has said what, based on what he or she can remember. If there is a difference in level between the person who is listening and those who are speaking, then some very useful recasting of utterances can occur with this activity. See Chapter 4 for more activities like these which work with the recycling and reactivation of texts.

How to find your way around this book

If you are looking for an activity involving memory to use with a class, then dipping into the first three chapters of this book is a good place to start. The activities here focus on the three basic memory processes of encoding, storage and retrieval. Chapter 1, *Mental stretching*, looks at the role of working memory in language processing and explores some ways of challenging learners to push their personal boundaries regarding how much language their own working memories can deal with. Chapter 2, *Making language memorable*, is about language storage and offers some ideas on how language can best be presented to learners so that it is linked with previous knowledge and becomes more memorable. Chapter 3, *Retrieving*, looks at some motivating and dynamic ways of getting learners to go back to what has been focused on in previous lessons.

In Chapter 4, *Repeating and reactivating*, we take a more long-term view of these processes and emphasize the importance of revisiting material. The activities in this chapter explore some ways of structuring exposure- and output-based classes so that the memory potential is maximized.

Sometimes teachers need to be proactive in encouraging active memorization of material, and the activities in the next two chapters help teachers to focus on this area. Chapter 5, *Memory techniques and mnemonics*, demonstrates a range of 'tricks' which have been used in many different fields for remembering things exactly and illustrates some ways of adapting them to language teaching. Chapter 6, *Learning by heart*, highlights some effective techniques and strategies for committing entire texts to memory.

Finally, Chapter 7, *Memory games*, examines some ways in which different memory processes may be activated using a game format.

Many of the activities in this book require very little in the way of materials or preparation. However, the support materials presented in the book are also available as PDF files on the CD-ROM accompanying this book. These can be projected in the classroom, or printed out and handed to your learners. For teachers who are interested in exploring further any of the ideas presented in *Memory Activities for Language Learning*, at the end of the book I have included short lists of reference works and websites that I have found especially helpful.

As already noted, there is a strong link between emotion and memorability, and many of the activities in this book are deliberately structured to engage the emotions of the language learners who will use them. For some learners, however, in certain situations, such activities may be inappropriate. It is important therefore that teachers are mindful of cultural sensitivities and exercise due discretion when choosing activities to use in class.

1 Mental stretching

As we have seen in the Introduction, many psychologists would now tend to focus less on the view of short-term memory as a *place* which language passes through on its way to long-term memory, or even as the *process* by which this happens, but instead as the *state* in which our brains may be temporarily, but actively and consciously, engaged with auditory, visual or spatial data. To emphasize the active role that it plays, the term *working memory* is now often preferred.

Much of what is currently believed about working memory originates with the multi-component model developed and made popular by the psychologist Alan Baddeley. It consists of a *central executive*, controlling three systems – the *phonological loop*, the *visual-spatial sketchpad* and the *episodic buffer* – which are called into play depending on the type of data being processed.

The phonological loop

If a person who is talking suddenly stops and asks us to repeat what they have been saying, the chances are that, even if we have not been paying close attention, we will be able to repeat the last few words of their utterance. This is known as *echoic memory*, and we use it by playing back to ourselves in our minds the words that we have just heard. Since echoic memory lasts for only a few seconds and has a very limited capacity, the amount of language processing that can happen is negligible. This may be the kind of memory that is employed by language learners when a short utterance of up to around six known words is drilled in class by the teacher. Of course, if some or all of the words in the utterance are unfamiliar to the learners, then the power of echoic memory is even more limited and the chances of accurate repetition are decreased.

This type of memory can be extended, however, by what is known as the *phonological loop*. Unlike echoic memory which is a largely subconscious activity, this system is more conscious and acts as a sort of inner internal conversation, where utterances are constantly repeated to oneself to avoid decay. We can observe this process happening when we say a phone number to ourselves over and over again until we manage to find a pen to write it down! The phonological loop allows for more language processing than echoic memory, and consequently we may be able to notice aspects of form and meaning, and create links with what is already retained in long-term memory.

Interestingly, the phonological loop is also employed as a mechanism to deal with written material. When we read a text, or indeed write one, recoding the visual input as auditory data and replaying it within the phonological loop allow us to understand the links between different ideas in what we are reading and, when we write, to produce text that is logically connected and coherent.

Many of the activities in this section will challenge learners to engage with this process.

The visual-spatial sketchpad

There is another way in which we can process visual data in working memory. In the same way that echoic memory allows immediate repetition of very short stretches of auditory data, *iconic memory* enables brief retention of visual material. Again, since it lasts for such a short period of time – less than a second in this case – processing of the image in any way is very limited. It is extended, however, through the *visual-spatial sketchpad*, which creates a sort of virtual world in the mind, temporarily generating images and allowing them to be manipulated and reflected on. This is the system we use when we have to think consciously about the route between two different places, or when we produce a drawing. The implications of this system for language learning may be less immediately obvious, but if it is combined with auditory material – when we try to explain the route to another person, for example, or, as in Activity 1.7: *Delayed TPR* (Total Physical Response) below, when we link an action with its name – the linguistic memory traces may be made stronger by its deployment.

The episodic buffer

Another form of multi-sensory processing of data may also occur in the *episodic buffer*. Here visual, auditory and spatial information is combined with information about chronological order into single episodic representations. It may be employed when we recall a scene from a film we have just seen, or the events of a story we have heard, as in Activity 1.12: *Reordered story* and Activity 1.13: *Co-constructed storytelling* at the end of this chapter. Recent evidence suggests that this kind of multi-sensory processing of information can leave longer-lasting memory traces, and indeed, the episodic buffer is thought to have very strong links with long-term memory.

An important point to remember about all of these systems is that they are severely limited by both time and capacity. External factors can also greatly diminish our working-memory abilities. Just think how difficult it can be to try to remember something or read while someone is asking you a question at the same time. Things are further complicated by the fact that we often overestimate how much of what is temporarily held in working memory will be retained later. There have been numerous occasions during the writing of this book when I have struggled to recall ideas I had had earlier, which, at the time, I was convinced I would remember without writing them down.

The capacity of working memory can be somewhat increased, however, through the process of *chunking*. If we take a telephone number such as 035689256, we can retain it more easily in working memory if we break it down into three units, 035–689–256, than if we attempt to remember each digit individually. This principle can also be applied to words, so a person who recognizes the chunks of language within the last sentence (*telephone number*, *more easily*, *working memory*, *break it down*, etc.) would have fewer difficulties retaining it than someone who did not.

There is also recent evidence to suggest that through training and practice, improvements in working memory can be made. Tracey Alloway's (2010) research would indicate not only that this is the case, but also that high working-memory levels in the young may be a better predicator of future academic success than traditional IQ tests. Thus, the activities in this chapter work with two ideas in mind. First, that encouraging learners to process language through their working memories is a useful step on the way to moving some of that language into long-term memory, and secondly that a well-trained working memory can help learners to develop in fluency, listening, reading, speaking and writing.

1.1 Flash!

Memory focus	Processing an image in working memory and using language to talk about it.
Level	Any
Time	10 minutes plus
Preparation	Find some interesting images that contain a fair amount of detail, such as a street scene (see an example in Box 1.1a) or the interior of a house (see an example in Box 1.1b). Prepare to display them with a projector or make them large enough so that they can be seen by the whole class. With a small class, it may be possible for each person to be given their own picture to work with.

Procedure

1   Organize the class into pairs. Show them the picture and ask the learners to talk to each other about what they can see. Be available to deal with vocabulary queries as they arise, and encourage dictionary use. For lower levels, you may want to remind them of how the structure *there is / there are* works. Now tell them that they need to try to remember as much as they can about the detail of the picture.

2   After about 30 seconds to a minute, ask one person in each pair to turn so that he or she can no longer see the picture.

3   The 'seeing' person in the pair now asks questions to see what their partner can remember. These questions will vary according to the level of the learners. For the picture in Box 1.1a, these could include: *How many people are in the picture? What is the old lady doing?*, etc.

4   Change roles and use another picture.

Box 1.1a: Flash!

From *Memory Activities for Language Learning*
© Cambridge University Press 2011

PHOTOCOPIABLE

Box 1.1b: Flash!

From *Memory Activities for Language Learning*
© Cambridge University Press 2011

PHOTOCOPIABLE

Variations

1   Show just one image for 30 seconds. Now dictate a series of true and untrue statements about the picture. If the statement is true, the learners write it down as it is. If it is not true, they need to adapt it to make it true, and then write it down. This idea is based on an activity in *Images* by Jamie Keddie, Oxford University Press, 2009.

2   Show the learners a short video (maximum one minute) from a video-sharing website such as You Tube™ (http://www.youtube.com). Both learners in each pair watch the video. One learner tries to remember as much detail as possible, while the other thinks of questions to ask the other (e.g. *What colour was the man's shirt?*). After they have asked and answered the questions, they watch the video again to check.

3   Instead of using a picture, display a grammar table (like the one for an elementary group in Box 1.1c) for a short time. Make sure no one is writing anything down. Now take the table away and ask them to work in pairs to write down as many correct sentences as they can, just using words from the table. (There are 19 possible questions from the table below.)

Box 1.1c: Flash!

How long	did you	stay	last night?
How much		eat	
When		go	
What		get here	
How		do	
Why		go home	

From *Memory Activities for Language Learning*
© Cambridge University Press 2011   PHOTOCOPIABLE

4   Display a short text or dialogue for a short period of time. Take it away
    and then ask the learners to write what they can from memory. Now
    ask them to work with a partner and to pool what they have written to
    produce their best version of the text together.

Drilling

Drilling in its basic format involves the teacher saying a word, phrase or
sentence in the form to be practised, and the learners repeating it. This
can be done chorally, with the whole class together, or individually, by
the teacher choosing the person to repeat. If the utterance is longer than
around seven or eight words, then working memory, as opposed to echoic
memory, will be employed to a certain extent, but simply repeating still
does not provide much in the way of cognitive challenge for learners. Here
are some variations on drilling which may help to make the process more
stimulating and meaningful, and consequently make the language being
practised more memorable.

Dramatic drilling

Changing the way in which the learners say the words may help to make the
language they are repeating more memorable. For instance, they could say
the items very slowly, quickly, quietly or loudly. They could also repeat them
in a way that reveals how they feel about the words: if the teacher is drilling
a list of food items, for example, they repeat the word in an enthusiastic
way if they like the foods, and in an unenthusiastic way if they do not.

Physical drilling

The teacher says the words while performing a physical action to make the
meaning clear. The learners repeat both the words and the physical action.
This works particularly well with a short story containing lots of action.

Who repeated?

The teacher stands with his or her back to the class and says a sentence in
the form to be practised. Someone in the class repeats the sentence. The
teacher tries to guess who it was who said it. If this is achieved, the person
who spoke now has a turn at being the person at the front and says another
sentence using the form.

1.2 Reversed drilling

Memory focus	Encouraging learners to process reformulated versions of their own utterances in working memory.
Level	Any
Time	5–15 minutes
Preparation	None

Procedure

1   When the learners are engaged in a freer speaking activity, listen in unobtrusively and make a note of some of the things that they are saying that could be improved upon.

2   Now write each utterance up on the board in a reformulated version, which makes it more accurate and/or uses more complex or clearer language. This should be done at a level which is not too far above the level of the learners. Give each utterance a number.

3   Bring everyone together and draw the learners' attention to the reformulated utterances on the board. Deal with any issues about meaning.

4   Now ask a learner to pick one of the utterances on the board. This could be either a reformulation of the learner's own utterance or the utterance of another learner. Ask him or her to say the utterance out loud. You now repeat the utterance in as natural a way as possible. The learner can now repeat the utterance as many times as desired. After each repetition, provide the learner with a natural model immediately.

Note

The idea for this activity comes from *Counseling-Learning: A Whole-Person Model for Education* by Charles A. Curran, New York: Grune and Stratton, 1972. Curran is the creator of community language learning (CLL) and coined the phrase 'Human Computer™' to refer to this approach to drilling.

1.3 The broken telephone

Memory focus	Providing practice in retaining long stretches of language in working memory.
Level	Elementary and above
Time	5–20 minutes (depending on the text)
Preparation	Choose a very short story or joke, suitable for the level of the group. Cut the text up into sections of one or two (if short) sentences. See the example in Box 1.3 for an intermediate group.

Procedure

1 Organize the class into groups of five to seven. Each group needs one set of the story sentences. These should be placed face down in order on the table next to the first person.

2 The first person in each group turns over the first piece of paper and whispers what it says to the next person in the group. The second person then whispers it to the next person, and so on. The last person, at the end of the line, writes down the sentence that he or she hears.

3 As soon as the first sentence has moved on from the second person, the first person can start whispering the second sentence to him or her, and so on. This way everyone is kept actively involved throughout the activity. When all of the sentences have passed down the line, the last person will end up with a complete version of the whole text.

4 Now ask each group to go through this version together, checking it for accuracy. Finally, they compare it with the original text and reflect on how any differences that they find occurred.

Box 1.3: The broken telephone

a) The Japanese eat very little fat and suffer fewer heart attacks than the British or Americans.

✂--

b) On the other hand, the French eat a lot of fat and also suffer fewer heart attacks than the British or Americans.

✂--

c) The Japanese drink very little red wine and suffer fewer heart attacks than the British or the Americans.

✂--

d) On the other hand the Italians drink lots of red wine and also suffer fewer heart attacks than the British or Americans.

✂--

e) The conclusion is 'Eat and drink what you like. It's speaking English that kills you!'

From *Memory Activities for Language Learning*
© Cambridge University Press 2011   PHOTOCOPIABLE

Variation

The first person whispers the sentences to the second person in English. The second person then mentally translates this sentence into the mother tongue and says the sentence in the mother tongue to the next person. The third person then translates back to English, etc. Of course, this version is only possible in a monolingual group.

1.4 Sentence swapping

Memory focus	Challenging learners to process a list of grammatically similar sentences in working memory.
Level	Elementary and above
Time	15 minutes
Preparation	Create or find 10 example sentences which use an area of language that you would like your class to focus on. Make enough copies of these so that there are enough for one per learner. See Box 1.4 for some examples using the 'double *the* + comparative' structure for an intermediate group.

Procedure

1   Give one sentence to each learner in the class. Make sure everyone understands what their sentence says.

2   Ask everyone to stand up so that they can move around freely. Everyone finds a partner and shares their sentences by saying them to each other. They now practise their partner's sentence until they can remember it exactly.

3   When they are both sure that they can do this, they move off and find a new partner. They now repeat the process, but this time using the sentence that they remembered from the previous partner.

4   The learners keep swapping partners and remembering new sentences until you feel that everyone has heard most of the sentences at least once. Of course, they may hear some of the sentences more than once. This doesn't matter – if this happens they still pass the sentence on to the next person they work with in the usual way.

5   Everyone sits down and writes down all of the sentences that they can remember. Now ask them to work in pairs and to correct and add to each other's lists.

6   Show the class the original list of sentences so that they can compare it with what they have written. They now go through the list in pairs, discussing which of the sentences they agree with and why.

Tip: It is important when setting this activity up to make it very clear that learners need to remember their partner's sentence each time they work with a new person. This is best done by demonstrating at the beginning with a few learners in front of the class.

Variations

1 For an extra challenge, ask learners to remember each new sentence that they hear as well all the other ones they have heard. Each time they meet a new person they repeat all of the sentences they can remember.

2 Find a short text of five to eight sentences. Give each learner in the class one of the sentences from the text. The activity works as above, but at the final stage they are trying to construct a complete text rather than a list of sentences.

Box 1.4: Sentence swapping

The more coffee you drink, the more tired you feel.

✂--

The more you talk about your feelings, the better your relationships are.

✂--

The more you learn other languages, the more open-minded you become.

✂--

The more exercise you get, the more energy you seem to have.

✂--

The more possessions you have, the more you want.

✂--

The later you have children, the more difficult it becomes to adapt.

✂--

The more freedom you give children, the more they start to behave badly.

✂--

The more mistakes you make, the more your English improves.

✂--

The more weapons a country has, the more likely it is to be involved in a war.

✂--

The smaller the class size, the more we can learn.

From *Memory Activities for Language Learning*
© Cambridge University Press 2011   PHOTOCOPIABLE

1.5 Working-memory challenge

Memory focus	Challenging learners to hold multiple new language items in working memory.
Level	Any
Time	5–15 minutes
Preparation	None

Procedure

1 Ask everyone to write down a list of six language items that they have learnt recently, or are struggling to learn or would like to learn. This could be single words, chunks or example sentences for an area of grammar. Allow plenty of time for this and encourage dictionary access, or help out by reformulating and correcting what they have written where necessary.

2 Now ask everyone to work with a partner and to swap lists.

3 Learner A now reads out two items from Learner B's list. Learner B repeats the items back in reverse order (i.e. repeating the second item and then the first). Learner A now repeats this process with three items, etc. What is the maximum number of items that Learner B can remember in reverse order?

4 Ask the learners to swap roles within their pairs and to give each other feedback, both on their ability to do the task and on the usefulness of the activity.

Variations

1 Make a list of sentences using a particular structure which get progressively longer (see the example below in Box 1.5). Learners work in pairs. Learner A looks at the sheet and reads out the sentences in order. Learner B listens and tries to repeat exactly the sentence that Learner A says. How far down the list can they get before it becomes too much to retain in working memory and they start making mistakes?

2 With a small class this activity can also be done as a competition. Divide the class into two groups. The teacher reads out the sentences in order and the members of each group take it in turns to repeat the sentences. Points are awarded according to how accurate the repetition was.

Box 1.5: Working memory challenge

I went to the shops. (5 words)

I bought a packet of rice. (6 words)

I had a shower in the morning. (7 words)

I played the guitar for a few hours. (8 words)

I listened to some music while I had breakfast. (9 words)

I made a cheese and tomato sandwich for my lunch. (10 words)

I watched a great football match on television in the evening. (11 words)

I wanted to swim in the sea but it was too cold. (12 words)

I cooked a really nice meal for everyone who lives in my house. (13 words)

I did some work in the garden and then came inside to have lunch. (14 words)

I tried to do some exercises in my grammar book, but they were very difficult. (15 words)

I went for a drink in a café with my brother and some of his friends. (16 words)

I had a delicious bowl of soup in a restaurant and then read some of my book. (17 words)

I took my little sister to school by car and then drove to my cousin's house for breakfast. (18 words)

I was really hungry, so I made lots of delicious pancakes and ate them all before everybody came home. (19 words)

I cleaned my house for three hours on Monday because it was very dirty after the party at the weekend. (20 words)

1.6 Waiters

Memory focus	Storing an increasingly lengthy list of food items in working memory and linking them to members of the class.
Level	Elementary and above
Time	5–20 minutes
Preparation	None

Procedure

1 Explain that you are a waiter and choose one of your learners to be your customer. Tell them that your customer is going to order a plate of food and a drink from you.

2 Go over to the customer and ask him what he would like to order. This could be anything he likes (within reason). Your task is to remember what he says.

> Customer: I'd like chicken and chips and a large glass of lemonade, please.
>
> Waiter: Would you like peas with that?
>
> Customer: Yes, please.
>
> Waiter: Ice in the lemonade?
>
> Customer: No, thanks.

3 Now walk right out of the room and immediately come back in again. Go back up to the customer and 'deliver' his food.

> Waiter: Here you are, sir. Chicken, chips and peas and a large glass of lemonade with no ice.
>
> Customer: Thanks very much.

4 Now hand the activity over to the learners and choose somebody to be the waiter. This time the waiter is going to repeat what you did, but this time with two customers. This is not a competition, however, and the task of the customer is not to try to make the waiter fail. Remember that the more dialogue that happens in each conversation (*Would you like sugar?*, etc.), the more likely the waiter is to succeed.

5 Keep changing the person who is the waiter and keep increasing the number of customer orders he or she has to remember each time. What is the maximum number of customer orders that anyone can remember?

1.7 Delayed TPR

Memory focus	Holding a list of instructions in working memory.
Level	Any
Time	5–15 minutes
Preparation	None

Procedure

1 Check that learners understand the vocabulary needed for the instructions that will be used (*pick up, carry, put down*, etc.) by asking individuals in the class to perform different actions (*pick up your pen*, etc.).

2 Give a list of instructions for a learner to follow, making sure that he or she starts to do the actions only after the list is complete. Start with only a few initially, but then build it up to see how many instructions learners can retain in memory at a time. Here are some examples for an elementary group:

> Go over to the whiteboard.
> Pick up the whiteboard marker.
> Draw a man on the board.
> Put the marker down in front of X.
> Take Y's pen.
> Give it to Z.
> Pull W out of her seat.
> Sit in her seat.
> Put her book on your head.
> Turn round.

3 Ask learners to do the same activity in pairs.

Follow-up

At the end of each sequence at Step 2, ask the other learners to recall the instructions that were followed. This is a natural way of activating past verb forms.

Note

There may be a marked difference in the number of instructions different learners can retain. For this reason it is better not to put learners on the spot too much in the whole-class format.

1.8 What did you say again?

Memory focus	Processing an area of grammar in working memory.
Level	Any
Time	5–15 minutes
Preparation	Plan some sentences about yourself that contain lots of examples of the structure to be focused on. See Box 1.8 for example sentences for beginner and upper intermediate groups.

Procedure

1 Read out the sentences at least once. The learners listen and try to remember as much information as possible. They should not make notes.

2 Ask the learners to work in pairs and tell each other as much as they can remember from what was said. They need to change the sentences from first to third person.

3 One learner tells the class what he or she can remember. The others and/or the teacher fill in any missing details.

4 The learners then do the same activity in pairs. Learner A tells Learner B lots of sentences about him- or herself using the forms. (They may need time and help to plan these first.) Learner B listens, tries to remember and then at the end repeats back everything he or she can recall. Learner B needs to change the sentences from first to second person.

5 Learners A and B then swap roles and repeat the process.

Box 1.8: What did you say again?

Beginners

My father is 84 years old.

My mother is 66 years old.

My older sister lives in London.

My younger sister is a teacher.

My older brother lives in Spain.

My younger brother lives in Devon.

Upper intermediate

I wish I hadn't given up playing rugby. If I hadn't given up I could've got quite good.

I wish I hadn't eaten so much last night. I feel really bloated this morning.

I wish I was more organized and didn't leave things to the last minute.

I wish I was better at getting out of bed in the morning.

I wish I'd learnt to drive when I was younger.

I wish I was rich enough to buy a big house with a garden where my kids could run around.

Note

This is a simple yet powerful language-recall activity. If the level of the speaker is higher, then the listener is nicely challenged to process new language. If the reverse is true, then the listener naturally reformulates what was said when he or she feeds back, and in doing so provides a gentle push to the speaker's own level.

1.9 The longest sentence

Memory focus	Challenging learners to retain a long sentence in working memory.
Level	Pre-intermediate and above
Time	5–15 minutes
Preparation	None

Procedure

1   Put the learners into groups of five to eight and ask them to stand in a circle or agree on an order between them. Their task is to create the longest sentence that they can as a group, with each person saying only one word at a time.

2   The first person in the group says one word. The next person now has to repeat the first person's word, and then say another which could follow it.

3   This process continues around the circle for as long as possible, with each person repeating the sentence as it stands up to that point, and then adding another word at the end.

4   If anyone feels that someone adds a word that is not possible, this should be discussed in the group and, if necessary, an alternative suggested. You need to be available to resolve any disagreements.

5   After about five minutes, ask each group to try to bring their sentence to a close.

6   Finally, ask one person from each group to tell you their sentence and write them up on the board. They can now be corrected if necessary and the class can comment on which is the longest / most interesting sentence, etc.

Note
I learnt this activity from Cecilia Orlandini, a teacher of teenagers in Italy.

1.10 Dialogue reconstruction

Memory focus	Holding sentences in working memory and then reconstructing them into a coherent dialogue.
Level	Any
Time	10–15 minutes
Preparation	Choose or write a six-line dialogue which is suitable for the level of the class. If using a projector, write each line on a separate PowerPoint® slide in a random order. Alternatively, write each line on a separate piece of paper that is large enough to see when held up in front of the class. See Box 1.10 for an example for an elementary group.

Procedure

1   Put the learners into groups of six and give each person in the group a number from 1 to 6. If the number of learners in the class does not divide into groups of six, two people in some of the groups can represent one number. Check that everyone is clear about who they are by asking all the '1's to raise their hands, etc.

2   Ask everyone to close their eyes except the '1's. Make sure nobody is cheating! Display one of the sentences (not the first one) and ask the '1's to try to remember it exactly. They should do this by holding it in working memory rather than by writing it down, of course! Remove the sentence. Now ask the '2's to open their eyes and everyone else to shut theirs. Display another of the sentences and ask the '2's to try to remember it exactly. Repeat this process with all of the sentences.

3   Now ask each group to try to reconstruct the six-line dialogue using all of the remembered sentences in the correct order.

4   Write the original dialogue on the board for them to compare with the reconstructed dialogue.

> ## Box 1.10: Dialogue reconstruction
>
> Did you have a good journey?
>
> ✂---
>
> Not bad, but I'm a bit tired.
>
> ✂---
>
> I'm sure you are! How long was the flight?
>
> ✂---
>
> Eleven hours, and the food was terrible.
>
> ✂---
>
> Really? Shall we get something to eat?
>
> ✂---
>
> That would be great!
>
> From *Memory Activities for Language Learning*
> © Cambridge University Press 2011   PHOTOCOPIABLE

Variation

Pin multiple copies of the lines of the dialogue randomly on the classroom walls. Learners work in pairs. One learner goes up to one of the sentences on the classroom wall, remembers it exactly, goes back to his or her partner (who has remained seated) and dictates the sentence to them. When six sentences have been collected in this way, each pair then tries to put all of the sentences into the correct order.

Follow-up

1   Once the complete dialogue is up on the board, drill it both chorally and individually, focusing on appropriate intonation. Now rub out some of the words and ask the learners to repeat the dialogue again. Gradually rub out more and more of the dialogue, until eventually the learners are repeating the dialogue with just a blank board to look at.

2   Learners engage in spontaneous conversations starting with *Did you have a good weekend/evening/party/meal/holiday?*, etc. They try to keep the conversation going for as long as possible.

1.11 Learner-generated texts

Memory focus	Encouraging learners to hold in working memory a text that has been co-constructed with them.
Level	Any
Time	20 minutes plus
Preparation	Choose a topic that the class could say some things about. This might be something that you know nothing about, such as a band that everybody likes, or the place where everybody lives. Find a picture of it if appropriate.

Procedure

1   Tell the class what the topic is and show the picture if you have one.

2   Ask for a volunteer from the class to say something about the topic. With a low-level group, this could be in the mother tongue. Now orally reformulate what was said to provide a more accurate or more sophisticated model. For instance, if a learner says *Near to here have many beaches very beautiful*, you could reformulate this as *There are a lot of really beautiful beaches nearby*. Write one word of the sentence on the board to stand as a memory aid for it, and then drill it around the room.

3   Try to construct about 10 different sentences with the learners. With each sentence, repeat the process of reformulating it, writing a word on the board to represent it, and then drilling it.

4   Keep reviewing everything by pointing at each word on the board, and asking the learners to recall the sentence it represents.

5   Finally ask everyone to write down all of the sentences as far as they can remember them. Do this yourself as well. The following sentences were produced when working with a group in Angola.

> Angola is rich in natural resources.
> Angola is a big country.
> Lots of different languages are spoken there.
> Angola has lots of oil and diamonds.
> Angola had a long civil war.
> Angola is at peace now.
> Angola is in South West Africa.
> Angola has a variety of different cultures.

6   Learners can now compare their sentences with each other's, and improve them where necessary.

7   Now ask one learner to write all of the sentences on the board. Can they now rewrite everything so that the sentences are linked to form a coherent text? Here is what one group in Angola produced from the sentences above.

> Angola is a big country in South West Africa. It is rich in natural resources like oil and diamonds. Lots of languages are spoken here and it has a variety of different cultures. It had a long civil war but is now at peace.

Note

This activity is based on Earl Stevick's 'Islamabad technique' (so called because it was first used as a way of producing a student-generated text about Islamabad). You can read about it in his seminal work, *Teaching Languages: A Way and Ways*, Heinle and Heinle, 1980, or in its re-edited and reissued format, *Working with Teaching Methods: What's at Stake?*, Heinle ELT, 1998. Instead of writing a word on the board for each utterance, you could also draw a symbol or simple image, or stick up a coloured piece of paper to represent it.

1.12 Reordered story

Memory focus	Challenging learners to hold the gist of a story in working memory, and to order it using their awareness of cohesive devices.
Level	Intermediate and above
Time	10–15 minutes
Preparation	Choose a story that can be broken down into no more than 10 short sections. Make a copy of the complete story for each learner in the class and one extra copy which has been cut up into slips. See Box 1.12 for an example for an intermediate group.

Procedure

1   Choose 10 learners to come to the front of the class. Give each learner randomly one of the slips from the story. Tell them the slips make up a story, but that it is in the wrong order. Their task as a whole group is to put the story in the correct order. No one may show their slip to anyone else.

2   Each person in turn reads out what is on their piece of paper in a
    loud, clear voice. Anyone can ask questions about language, but try
    to encourage the class to deal with these queries themselves, wherever
    possible, without intervention from you.
3   Anyone can now make suggestions as to the order of the story. The
    learners at the front move themselves according to the order suggested.
4   Keep encouraging them to tell the story from the beginning and to move
    themselves around until everyone is happy with the order.
5   Learners work in pairs and retell the story as they remember it.
6   Finally give out the complete story to everyone.

Variation

Divide the class into groups of 10 and give each group a set of the slips. They
try to put themselves in the correct order as quickly as possible, but again
without showing their slips to anyone else. With classes that will not divide
into 10 exactly, sentence 5 can be taken out and/or two learners can share
the same slip. For more examples of texts that can be used in this way, see
'Teacherless tasks', in *More Grammar Games* by Paul Davis and Mario
Rinvolucri, Cambridge University Press, 1995.

Follow-up

Learners write an ending for the story.

Box 1.12: Reordered story

Gunesh was furious to think that everything was over. That Ayo didn't love her any more and had found somebody else.

✂---

As she packed up her things in the bedroom, her eyes fell upon the bed and an idea came into her head.

✂---

She went to the kitchen and took out a packet of frozen prawns from the freezer.

✂---

Back in the bedroom she took off the four bed posts, poured the prawns inside, and then replaced the posts again.

✂---

She phoned Ayo on her mobile. 'The flat is all yours,' she said.

✂---

Ayo and Lee moved in that afternoon. They were pleased to see that Gunesh hadn't taken the bed with her.

✂---

Time passed, and they couldn't help noticing a strange smell in the bedroom, which seemed to be getting worse.

✂---

After a few months it was unbearable, and neither of them could work out where it was coming from.

✂---

Eventually they decided they could stand it no longer. Ayo phoned Gunesh to say they were moving out. Would she like to buy the flat from them at a reduced rate?

✂---

Gunesh accepted and went round to get the keys. She smiled to herself as she saw the removal men carefully lifting the bed into the removal van.

From *Memory Activities for Language Learning*

PHOTOCOPIABLE

1.13 Co-constructed storytelling

Memory focus	Challenging learners to hold the spoken utterances of a story in working memory.
Level	Any
Time	5–20 minutes (depending on the story)
Preparation	Choose a story that your class will find interesting and that has a substantial dialogue content. Alternatively, use the example in Box 1.13, which is pitched at a pre-intermediate group.

Procedure

1 Choose volunteers to play each of the characters in the story and invite them to the front of the class. For the story in Box 1.13, you will need five people to play the five characters of the man, the wolf, the tree, the young woman and the wise old woman who lives at the end of the world. The rest of the class simply watch the story.

2 Tell the story, adapting it to suit the level of the group you are working with. Each time there is a line of dialogue, say what the character says, and then indicate that the person playing that role should repeat the line. Encourage them to do it as naturally as possible, adapting the level of the lines to suit the learners. It also helps to break the dialogue up into short manageable chunks before they repeat it. The actors should move around the stage as the story demands it.

Follow-up

Give out the text of the story and ask the learners to do the same activity in groups of six. One person in each group (a stronger learner) takes on the role of storyteller.

Note

I learnt the idea of learners repeating and performing the dialogue content of this story from the storyteller Michael Quinn, who has used it with mixed-nationality groups of adults at the Totnes School of English.

Box 1.13: Co-constructed storytelling

The unluckiest man in the world

Once upon a time the unluckiest man in the world was sitting on a bench. 'Why does everything I do go wrong?' he asked himself. 'I've lost my job. I've lost my girlfriend, I've lost my home – I've lost everything!' Then he had an idea. 'I'll walk to the end of the world and I'll ask the wise old woman how to get some luck.'

So he started on his journey to the end of the world. After walking for a while, he came to a forest and there he saw a wolf. The wolf looked very sad and very thin and very hungry. 'What's wrong with you?' said the man.

'I don't know what to do,' said the wolf. 'I feel so weak and tired and hungry all the time and I don't know why.'

'Well,' said the man, 'I'm going to the end of the world to ask the wise old woman how to get some luck. If you want I could ask her why you're so hungry.'

'I would be very grateful,' said the wolf, and the man continued on his journey.

After a while he came to a tree. The tree looked very small and sad, and all of its leaves were missing – even though it was the middle of summer.

'What's wrong with you?' said the man.

'I don't know what to do,' said the tree. 'I can't grow. All of the other trees get bigger and bigger but I just stay the same.'

'Well,' said the man, 'I'm going to the end of the world to ask the wise old woman how to get some luck. If you want I could ask her why you can't grow.'

'Oh, thank you so much,' said the tree, and the man continued on his journey.

When he was nearly at the end of the world, he came to a lovely house, and standing at the front door was a very beautiful young woman. 'Come inside!' she called to him. 'You must be hungry after your journey,' and she cooked him a wonderful meal with delicious wine and they laughed and joked together. But then the young woman suddenly started to cry.

'What's wrong?' said the man.

'I don't know what to do,' said the young woman. 'I'm so sad and lonely living here on my own, and I don't know why.'

'Well,' said the man, 'I'm going to the end of the world to ask the wise old woman how to get some luck. If you want I could ask her why you are so sad and lonely.'

continued

Box 1.13: (*cont.*)

'Oh, thank you,' said the young woman. 'You are so kind.' And the man continued on his journey.

And finally he got to the end of the world and there was the wise old woman sitting on a cloud. 'What do you want?' asked the wise old woman.

'I want to know where my luck is,' replied the man.

'It's right in front of you,' said the wise old woman. 'You just have to recognize it.'

'Oh, I see,' said the man. 'Thanks very much.' And the man was just about to go when he remembered the questions of his friends. He listened as the wise old woman whispered the answers to him, and when she was finished he started to walk home again.

He got to the house of the beautiful young woman. 'The wise old woman said you need to find a husband to live with you,' he called to her. 'Then you won't be sad and lonely.'

'I see,' said the young woman. 'Would you like to be my husband? You could live with me in this lovely house and I'll cook for you every day and massage your feet.'

'I'm sorry,' said the man, 'I have to go and find my luck. The wise old woman said it's right in front of me. I just have to recognize it. Sorry.'

And he continued on his journey. When he got to the forest, the tree said to him, 'Did you find out what is wrong with me?'

'Yes,' said the man. 'The wise old woman said there is a box of treasure under your roots. You need to find somebody to dig it up so that your roots can grow again.'

'Could you dig it up?' said the tree. 'You can keep the treasure.'

'I'm sorry,' said the man. 'I have to go and find my luck. The wise old woman said it's right in front of me. I just have to open my eyes and see it. Sorry.' And he continued on his journey.

Soon he came to the wolf, lying on the ground, almost dead. 'Did you ask the wise old woman for me?' said the wolf.

'Yes,' replied the man. 'The wise old woman said you are hungry because you're not eating enough. To feel better you just have to eat the first stupid man who comes your way!'

And that is exactly what he did!

2   Making language memorable

Working memory allows for immediate processing of material that we are exposed to in the short term. At some point, however, we need more than this. We need something to happen to this material so that it gets stored in long-term memory for retrieval when required. We need to make language memorable. Where working memory is limited by both time and capacity, long-term memory is seemingly limitless. But we know from experience that everything in working memory does not automatically get stored in long-term memory: in fact, only a very small percentage of what we perceive through the senses is available for exact retrieval at a later stage. Neither is it certain that what has entered long-term memory will remain available indefinitely. There may be things that we remember for an entire lifetime, for a month, for a week or for just a day.

So what is it that determines whether something is going to get stored or not? Long-term memory is not an empty vessel that can have language simply poured into it. In fact, the existing contents of memory are an essential component in new memory storage. If we view our memories as a dynamic network of ideas, interacting with each other in multi-faceted formats, then the more ways in which new language can be linked to what is already there and included in the interactions, the more effective the storage will be. It is rather like a new student joining a class. The more quickly that person is able to interact with the other students and find things in common, the more quickly he or she will feel welcome and want to stay. Here are some of the factors that may be instrumental in making language 'feel welcome' in our long-term memories, and that are an integral feature of the activities which follow.

Repetition

This has been identified as the single most important factor in making language memorable. Research suggests that we may need to meet a language item up to 16 times before it is fixed in long-term memory. The more we encounter a language item, and the more often we are called upon to use it, the more readily it will become part of our repertoire. This process could occur naturally, because the word is high frequency, or artificially, because learners are deliberately provided with activities that challenge them to understand or to use it. Of course, it is not just a matter of parroting the word over and over again. Repetition should also occur in ways that are varied and meaningful to the learners.

Personalization

If learners are able to link the new language to their own lives in some way, by using it to talk about themselves, their experiences, their future plans, or those of people they know, it is much more likely to stick. Not only is this more motivating for learners, but since this is a very common way in which language is used, it is also more likely that the language will get recycled in similar ways again.

Motivation

It is difficult to remember something that we do not see any need for. There is a strong link between motivation and personalization, but there are many other reasons why some language items may be more motivating than others. We may see some words or structures as being more important than others, for instance, perhaps because of an exam or the need to study language related to a particular field.

Chunking

Much of an advanced language user's mental lexicon is made up of the typical patterns of language: the company that words keep, rather than individual words. If we draw learners' attention to chunks of language, and encourage them to do so themselves, it is more likely that they will be stored as whole entities (perhaps with links to similar patterns) and retrieved as whole entities later as required.

Associations

As well as remembering language in patterns, we also remember words because of the links that exist with other words already in our mental lexicons. The more associations that a word has, the more likely we are to be able to retain it. These associations could be related to the meaning of the word (*cat – dog, milk, purr*, etc.) or form (*cat – sat, fat, rat*, etc.).

Contextualization

Vocabulary and grammar are more memorable if they are anchored in a particular context of use. Wherever possible, language should be presented and practised in texts, rather than at a purely word or sentence level, so that its pragmatic meaning (rather than simply its semantic meaning) is obvious. Exploring the typical intonation patterns of spoken language in such texts will also help with this process.

Affective factors

There are strong links between emotion and memory. If something makes us feel happy or upset, gives us the giggles or shocks us, the language that occurs around this situation tends to stick a bit more easily. Just think how comparatively easy it is to remember how to say 'I love you,' or a series of swear words in another language! Somewhat in contrast to the last category, we also sometimes find language more memorable when it is used in creative, unusual or even silly ways.

Physicality

Many actors find that they can remember their lines more easily if they can link them to a particular way of standing, or a movement across the stage. If learners can associate a particular area of language with a gesture or another movement that somehow illustrates the meaning, then this can also be a stimulus for the area of language to be remembered. It has also been shown that brief bouts of physical exercise can lead to better concentration and enhanced attention, both essential requirements for remembering new language.

Decision making

Every time we make a decision about a word, we are forging links with existing long-term memory knowledge. These decisions could be to do with language form ('Think of some words which rhyme with this word'), or meaning ('Write the word next to the person it applies to'). Encouraging learners to also talk about the decisions they have made will also help to reinforce the memorability of language items.

2.1 Memory strategies share

Memory focus	Encouraging learners to reflect on the strategies they use for remembering new words in another language, and to share these strategies with others.
Level	Any (for lower levels, the discussion parts of this activity may take place in the mother tongue)
Time	Short periods of 2–10 minutes over the course of a lesson
Preparation	Prepare a word list of about 10 unrelated language items which will be new for the learners. Write the mother-tongue equivalent next to each word. See the possible example for an elementary group with Brazilian Portuguese translations in Box 2.1a. For multilingual classes, you will need to use pictures (e.g. the household tools on page 145) or a paraphrase for each word.

Procedure

1 Give out the word list to each learner. Say each of the English words so that learners can hear the pronunciation. Now ask everyone to study it, and to try to remember each word in English and its meaning. Tell them that you will test them on the words later on in the class. Do not allow anyone to write anything down.

2 Now take the lists away from them and do something completely unrelated.

3 At a later point in the lesson, return to the words by writing on the board just the mother-tongue versions. Ask everyone to try to recall the English equivalent for each one. When everyone has had a chance to do this, give them back the word list so that they can check their answers.

4 Take the lists away again and continue with another unrelated activity.

5 Finally, ask everyone to work in small groups and, without any prompts, see how many of the English words they can recall now. Do the learners think they will also be able to remember the words tomorrow / in a week's time? Ask them to discuss and compare any strategies that they used to remember each word.

6   Ask each group to share their best strategies with the rest of the class.
    Some areas to focus on might include:
    - repeating the word to yourself
    - trying to create an image to remember the word by
    - linking the word to its meaning, or another word in the mother tongue
    - trying to put the word into context somehow
    - challenging yourself to recall the word in a test
    - personalizing the word in some way.

Box 2.1a: Memory strategies share

yawn (verb)	*bocejar*
worm (noun)	*verme*
untidy (adjective)	*desorganizado, desordenado*
knowledge (noun)	*conhecimento*
ruin (verb)	*arruinar, destruir*
hail (noun)	*chuva de pedregulhos de gelo, granizo*
suddenly (adverb)	*de repente*
retired (adjective)	*aposentado*
burp (noun)	*arroto*
polish (verb)	*polir / tornar luzidio*

Variation

The strategies in Box 2.1b were suggested by Year 10 pupils (aged 14–15) at
All Saints RC School, York. Give the sheet out to the learners for them to
read. Ask everyone to go through it and underline everything that they think
is a good idea. They then share and discuss in small groups what they have
underlined.

Box 2.1b: Memory strategies share

How do I remember new words in French?

The way I remember French vocabulary is by listening to a recording of the words while I read them on a sheet in front of me. This way I can link the sound of the word with the written form. (*Dom*)

If I want to remember a few sentences in French, I read them through a few times, then I cover them up and try to say them to myself and write them down without looking at the originals. Finally I uncover the sentences and see if what I wrote is correct. I keep doing this until I definitely know the sentences. (*Melissa*)

I think of words that sound like the French word and then imagine a picture linking the two things. Here's an example:

 Car c'est génial (Because it's great). (*Felix*)

I go over the words before I go to bed and then try to remember them again first thing in the morning when I wake up. (*Danl*)

To memorize new words, I usually draw pictures of the things I have to learn. I also write the words out over and over again and say them to myself. I think I remember words better if I hear myself saying them. (*Ruby*)

I only try to learn about five words at a time. Little and often works better for me. (*Chloe*)

I have to sit in a very quiet place and then I ask my mum to test me on what I've been learning. (*Callum*)

The best thing to do is go on the internet and play a few games which use the words. This really helps to get the words into my head. (*Selina*)

I have to put the words into a sentence and then say them over and over again. (*Scarlett*)

If I can think of a word that rhymes with the word, it really helps me to remember it. (*Eden*)

(Strategies supplied by Year 10 pupils at All Saints RC School, York)

From *Memory Activities for Language Learning*
© Cambridge University Press 2011   PHOTOCOPIABLE

2.2 Word knowledge

Memory focus	Making language memorable by encouraging learners to store as much information as necessary about it. Sharing ideas about what information to store.
Level	Intermediate and above
Time	20 minutes plus
Preparation	None

Procedure

1   Write the word *worth* on the board and next to it write the translation into the mother tongue of the class. If working in a multilingual context, write a translation into a language that you know.

2   Establish that having a translation of the word is unlikely to be enough to enable students to use the word successfully if they did not know the word before. Elicit what else they would need to know about it, focusing on the issues below and presenting them as a spidergram (see Box 2.2).

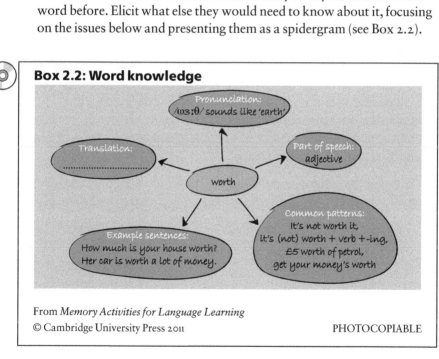

Box 2.2: Word knowledge

Pronunciation:
/wɜːθ/ sounds like 'earth'

Translation:
....

Part of speech:
adjective

worth

Common patterns:
It's not worth it,
it's (not) worth + verb +-ing,
£5 worth of petrol,
get your money's worth

Example sentences:
How much is your house worth?
Her car is worth a lot of money.

From *Memory Activities for Language Learning*
© Cambridge University Press 2011   PHOTOCOPIABLE

3 Now ask everyone individually to write down all five elements in order of importance for them. They then compare and discuss their lists in pairs or small groups.

4 Bring everyone together and encourage people to share opinions about which of the elements they feel are the most important in terms of helping them to remember and use new language. Where time is limited, which elements would they include in their vocabulary notebook?

2.3 Word patterns share

Memory focus	Helping to make some key word patterns memorable through independent research and peer teaching.
Level	Intermediate and above
Time	30–45 minutes
Preparation	Make sure that some or all of the sources outlined in Step 2 are available.

Procedure

1 Write the word *thing* on the board. Elicit from the class some common language patterns that use this word and write them around it as illustrated in Box 2.3. Check understanding of the patterns by establishing personalized examples for each one.

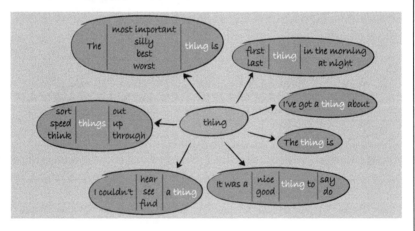

Box 2.3: Word patterns share

From *Memory Activities for Language Learning*
© Cambridge University Press 2011   PHOTOCOPIABLE

2   Now give each pair of learners a key word and ask them to find patterns for it. Some examples could be *back, get, give, good, just, keep, mean, put, own, still, stop, take, then, want, work*. Ask them to find around eight useful patterns for their word and to write them out in a 'map' like your example on the board. Both members of the pair should create one. There are three main sources that they could use for doing this:
    * a monolingual or good bilingual dictionary (many of which will contain multiple entries for these words)
    * *Natural Grammar: The Keywords of English and How They Work* by Scott Thornbury, Oxford University Press, 2004, a book focusing on the common patterns of 100 key words of English
    * an online collocation site such as http://forbetterenglish.com/

    The learners need to understand the patterns that they are writing down and should be prepared to provide a personalized example for each one. Be available to deal with queries when they arise.
3   Now rearrange the class so that learners from different pairs are working together. Ask them to show their maps and to teach each other the patterns and personalized examples that they found.
4   Display their maps on the walls of the class so that everyone has a chance to see them all.

Follow-up

Encourage learners to keep their own notebooks where they record examples of the patterns they have identified, as well as the new ones they later encounter.

2.4 Associations

Memory focus	Making language items memorable by forging links with other words in long-term memory.
Level	Any
Time	5 minutes plus
Preparation	Prepare a list of unrelated language items to be reviewed.

Procedure

1   Slowly read out the items you have planned to review. After each one, ask learners to write down, individually, the first word or phrase that comes into their heads that they associate with it. Emphasize that they should write down only this – not the word itself.

2 Ask the learners, in pairs, to use what they have written down to recall the original words. The learners also discuss and compare the different associations they made between the words.

Follow-up
Learners go back to their lists in a later class and try to recall the words again.

Variations
1 Instead of writing down a word association, learners write down what they perceive to be the opposite of the language item. You may need to do a few examples with everyone first to establish that deciding on opposites is a subjective process. What is the opposite of *table*, for example? Is it *floor* or *in a mess* or *boat*?
2 Word associations can also be used as an activity for groups of learners standing in a circle. Each person takes it in turn to say a word that they associate with what the previous person said. At the end of the activity, they can often recall the complete list of language items used by going backwards round the circle.

2.5 Real or imagined?

Memory focus	Making spoken utterances memorable by encouraging learners to visualize a personalized context in which they may be used.
Level	Pre-intermediate and above
Time	10 minutes
Preparation	None

Procedure
1 Write a list of spoken utterances on the board which it would be useful for the class to know. See the examples below.

You must be joking.	I need to talk to you.
It's not my fault.	I've had enough of this.
Wow! That's amazing!	Hurry up!
It's not good enough.	What have you done?
I can't believe it.	I'm so sorry.
That's very kind of you.	Can you do me a favour?

2   Check that everyone understands all the utterances by using translation and/or establishing a context in which each utterance might be made.

3   Ask everyone to choose three or four of the utterances and to remember a context in which either they said the utterance or it was said to them. The conversation could have taken place in English or in their mother tongue, but they should visualize it happening in English. If they cannot think of real contexts, ask them to imagine a few contexts in which some of the utterances could have been said.

4   Learners now share their contexts in small groups. Those who are listening try to guess which of the contexts are things that really happened.

Follow-up
Each group chooses one or two of the contexts to present as role plays to the others.

2.6 Well … this is my granddad

Memory focus	Making vocabulary memorable through personalization and visualization.
Level	Elementary and above
Time	20 minutes plus
Preparation	The teacher needs to plan a list of words and expressions to be focused on. This activity is an ideal way of activating and personalizing language for describing people but can also be used for likes and dislikes, activities or any other vocabulary area that can be linked to a person. See Box 2.6 for some examples for different levels.

Procedure

1   Quickly draw a picture of an important person in your life on the board. This person may be living or dead. Around the drawing add a few pictures of what that person is/was interested in or involved with. The quality of drawing does not matter. In fact, for the purposes of this exercise it is probably better if the drawing is not a work of art!

2   Tell the group about your person in as much detail as appropriate, using the pictures as a point of reference.

3   Ask the learners to do a quick drawing of an important person in their lives and to include drawings of things that that person is interested in.

4   Now ask them to talk about their people in pairs, referring to their pictures.

5   Dictate the words and expressions to be focused on to the class (see Box 2.6). With a small group, where you have been able to monitor Step 4, you may wish to adapt this focus slightly to suit specific needs. If the learners think that the word dictated applies to their person, they should write it close to their drawing of him or her. If it does not apply (or if they do not know what it means), they write it a long way away from the picture. As you dictate, write the words up yourself in the appropriate place on the board, thinking about the person you originally drew.

6   Talk about your person again, this time using the words that were dictated and trying to include examples in his or her speech to remind the learners of meanings. For example: *A good laugh? No I wouldn't say he was a good laugh. He's quite a serious person, actually. He doesn't really make many jokes.*

7   Ask the learners to do the same thing in pairs, preferably with a different partner from the previous exercise.

Variations

1   Instead of solely dictating the words yourself, invite suggestions from the class for words or chunks that could be used.

2   Ask the learners to draw pictures of two different people. They write the words closest to the person they most apply to.

3   Instead of a person, learners can draw a place they know really well, or an event that they have witnessed or experienced.

Box 2.6: Well ... this is my granddad

Elementary	Intermediate	Advanced
strong	cheeky	a good laugh
cleaning the house	untidy	a bit of a gossip
kind	a good listener	quite witty
the garden	sensitive	the outdoor type
shy	quite sensible	the life and soul of the party
a morning person	DIY	pretty ambitious
quiet	stubborn	an addictive personality

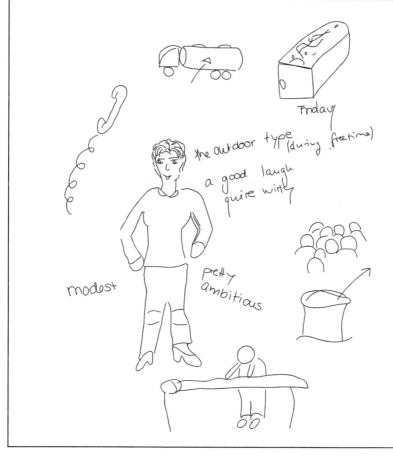

2.7 Pictorial links

Memory focus	Encouraging learners to store new language by creating strong links with visual images.
Level	Elementary and above
Time	10 minutes plus
Preparation	Make one double-sided copy of the picture in Box 2.7 for each learner.

Procedure

1   Ask learners to write a list of new language items from a text they have read, or from the audioscript in the back of their coursebooks. This could be either for homework or in class.

2   Give out copies of the picture. Ask everyone to think of some ways in which they could link one of the language items to something in the picture. For example, for the word *concentrate*, you could say *The cow was concentrating hard on drinking from the river*.

3   Now ask everyone to find their own links between each of the words and something in the picture, and then write the word next to it.

4   Everyone now compares pictures with the person next to them and explains the links they made.

5   At a later stage in the lesson (or on a different day), ask everyone to turn over their pieces of paper (where there is a clean copy of the picture) and to try to recall the language items that go with each part of the image. Can they also do this without looking at the image?

Follow-up
Learners bring in their own photographs or pictures to create links with other language items.

Note
I learnt this technique from Celal Yilmaz, a teacher of English for tourism in Turkey.

Making language memorable

Box 2.7: Pictorial links

From *Memory Activities for Language Learning*
© Cambridge University Press 2011

2.8 A silly love story

Memory focus	Creating a silly and memorable context in which to reactivate areas of language from the coursebook.
Level	Pre-intermediate and above
Time	15 minutes
Preparation	A plastic bag and 23 small slips of paper. If there are more than 23 learners in the class, then provide enough slips for one per learner.

Procedure

1   Share out the slips of paper among the learners, making sure that everyone has at least one.
2   Ask them to copy out a sentence from the unit of the coursebook that you have just been using. This could be something chosen entirely at random. They should remember exactly what they have written.
3   Collect in the slips and mix them around in the plastic bag.
4   Four volunteers are needed to take on the roles of Juliet, Romeo, Juliet's father and Romeo's mother. Juliet and her father should stand at the front right, facing the rest of the class, while Romeo and his mother should stand at the front left. Juliet picks 9 slips of paper randomly from the bag, Romeo picks 6, Juliet's father 5, and Romeo's mother 3.
5   The teacher begins to tell the story (see Box 2.8). The characters should move around as the events unfold. Whenever their character has to speak, they read out what is written on one of their slips of paper. When the wedding guests speak, towards the end of the story, the learners who are not acting in the story say what they originally wrote on their slips of paper. They do this all at once so that it sounds like a noisy crowd.

Note

Instead of using sentences from the coursebook, ask learners to write well-formed sentences using a particular tense or other area of grammar. Alternatively, they could produce sentences that are related to a particular topic (e.g. food). The idea for this activity comes from the work of Andrew Wright.

Box 2.8: A silly love story

Once upon a time there was a girl called Juliet who was very, very bored. Every day and every night she sat in her room staring out of the window. Her father was worried about her. He brought her nice food and said things to try to cheer her up: '…' But she was still bored and she just said '…'

One evening the moon was shining exceptionally brightly through her curtains. She went over to the window, opened it and stared out. She said sadly to herself '…' as she looked up at the moon. Suddenly she saw a boy standing in the street. He was really good-looking. His name was Romeo. She said to herself '…'

Romeo heard what she said. He looked up and saw her. Their eyes met and it was love at first sight. He walked up to her window and called up to her romantically '…' Juliet replied romantically '…' Romeo started to climb up the drainpipe. He said '…' passionately. Juliet was worried he might fall. She called out '…'

Suddenly Juliet's father came into the room. He shouted angrily '…' Romeo fell from the drainpipe. As he hit the ground, he said '…' and ran home as fast as he could. Juliet was angry with her father for scaring Romeo away. She shouted at him '…' Juliet's father was sorry for scaring away Romeo. He said '…'

Juliet went to sleep. She started dreaming about Romeo. She started talking in her sleep. '…' she said. Juliet's father was worried about her. He said '…' Meanwhile Romeo was dreaming about Juliet as well. He started talking in his sleep too. '…' he said. Romeo's mother was worried about him. She said '…'

Suddenly Romeo got up and started sleepwalking. He went out of his bedroom, out of his house and started walking slowly back to Juliet's house. His mother was following him. She was very worried. She said '…' to try to wake him. But Romeo just carried on sleeping and walking. Finally he got to Juliet's house. He woke up and called up to her window '…' Juliet woke up and answered back '…'

They decided to get married. They invited all their friends to come and celebrate with them. Juliet's father made a very proud speech at the wedding '…' All the guests said to each other '…' Romeo's mother announced to all the guests '…' All the guests cheered '…'

Romeo looked into Juliet's eyes and said '…' Juliet looked into Romeo's eyes and said '…' And all the guests cheered loudly '…' And they all lived happily ever after.

From *Memory Activities for Language Learning*

2.9 Emotional chants

Memory focus	Making vocabulary memorable through exploring its emotional value.
Level	Beginner–elementary
Time	15 minutes
Preparation	None

Procedure

1 Ask the learners to stand up where they have space to move around a little.

2 Tell them that together you are going to chant the days of the week. For each of the days they should show their exaggerated feelings about it, through tone of voice, body language and gestures. Student reactions to the different days of the week may vary, but Monday to Friday could be said miserably, looking down at the ground, and Saturday and Sunday could be cheered in a very enthusiastic way, and with appropriate gestures. Go through the sequence a few times with everyone, walking around the class in a circular motion if possible.

3 Now assign a vocabulary area to each group of up to eight learners. Depending on the level and interests of the learners, these could include food and drink, activities in the home, the weather, sports, pop groups, football teams, school subjects, films, etc.

4 Their task now is to produce an emotional chant for this area of vocabulary. They need to first agree on which items to include and then decide how each of the items will be said. They then practise the chant in their groups before performing it for the rest of the class.

2.10 Celebrity rhyming poems

Memory focus	Making the pronunciation of language items memorable through encouraging learners to create links between words with similar sounds.
Level	Pre-intermediate and above
Time	10 minutes plus
Preparation	Choose some names of celebrities and words that rhyme with them which are appropriate for your learners. The examples in Box 2.10a cover many of the common vowel sounds in English. For more examples, consult an online rhyming dictionary such as http://www.rhymezone.com/

Procedure

1 Depending on the level of the group, dictate one or both of the two verses or write it up on the board. Check that everyone understands the meaning and recognizes the rhyme between the last words of each line.

He's Barack Obama   He's Barack Obama
He doesn't like drama   He's a bit of a charmer
He works as a farmer   He wears special armour
He's wearing pyjamas   It makes him feel calmer
He's Barack Obama   He's Barack Obama

2 Give each learner or small group the name of a different celebrity plus a list of words which rhyme with the surname. (See Box 2.10a for some examples.)

3 Ask them to produce short poems, which follow the same structure as the example, using the name and some of the rhyming words that they have been given. Emphasize that the poems do not need to be true and can be as silly as they like.

4 Ask learners to display the poems around the room or read them out for the rest of the class to enjoy. Here's one created by two learners in an intermediate class.

When I see Tom Cruise
I get a bit confused
But I bought new shoes
So he can't refuse
I'm the girl he'll choose!
(By Camille Chardon and Vera Sevastyanova)

Note

The context in which you work will determine the most appropriate choice of celebrity names to use. It is of course also possible to simply give the learners a list of rhyming words and ask them to compose a poem with them.

Variation

Give each pair of learners one of the lexical chunks from Box 2.10b and ask them to write a rhyming poem with the chunk as the first and last line. Here is an example using 'By the way'.

> By the way
> I want to say
> That from today
> I'm going to stay
> By the way

Box 2.10a: Celebrity rhyming poems

Dick Cheney	/eɪ/ and /iː/	brainy/grainy/rainy/zany
Brad Pitt	/ɪ/	bit/fit/grit/hit/kit/knit/lit/pit/sit/spilt/spit/wit
Ronnie Wood	/ʊ/	could/good/hood/should/stood/would
Tom Cruise	/uː/	blues/bruise/choose/confuse/excuse/lose/news/refuse/shoes/snooze/stews/use/views
George Best	/e/	arrest/best/chest/depressed/detest/dressed/guessed/guest/nest/obsessed/pest/protest/request/rest/stressed/suggest/test
Christina Aguilera	/eə/ and /ə/	can't bear her/carer/compare her/ fairer/dare her/prepare her/scare her/wearer
Damien Hirst	/ɜː/	burst/cursed/dispersed/first/nursed/rehearsed/reversed/thirst/worst
Jude Law	/ɔː/	adore/before/bore/chore/door/draw/drawer/explore/for/four/ignore/more/pour/rapport/roar/score/shore/snore/sore/war/wore/your

continued

Box 2.10a: (*cont.*)

Johnny Cash	/æ/	ash/bash/clash/crash/dash/rash/ smash/thrash
Tom Hanks	/æ/	banks/planks/pranks/spanks/tanks/ thanks
Barack Obama	/ɑː/ and /ə/	armour/calmer/charmer/drama/farmer/ karma/pyjamas
Courteney Cox	/ɒ/	blocks/box/knocks/crocs/locks/rocks/ shocks/socks/stocks
Britney Spears	/ɪə/	beers/cheers/ears/fears/hears/gears/ tears/years
Bill Gates	/eɪ/	dates/greats/hates/mates/plates/rates/ states/weights
Michael Caine	/eɪ/	again/brain/champagne/complain/drain/ entertain/explain/ insane/pain/plane/ rain/Spain/stain/train
Danny Boyle	/ɔɪ/	aluminium foil/coil/loyal/oil/royal/soil/ spoil
Sharon Stone	/əʊ/	alone/bone/blown/clone/flown/grown/ loan/moan/ phone/postpone/thrown/ zone
Mariah Carey	/eə/ and /iː/	canary/contrary/dairy/fairy/hairy/scary
Stephen Fry	/aɪ/	buy/cry/deny/die/dry/fly/ give it a try/ goodbye/guy/ high/July/reply/shy/sky/ spy/supply/why
Gordon Brown	/aʊ/	around/clown/crown/down/drown/ frown/noun/town

From *Memory Activities for Language Learning*
© Cambridge University Press 2011

Box 2.10b: Celebrity rhyming poems

It's not worth it	It's up to you	Have a go	Just in time
By any chance	If you ask me	Just as well	All day long
Where've you been?	The last but one	By the way	Have a drink
I know what you mean	Come what may	Never mind	One by one
Whatever you want	If you like	From now on	Too bad
I couldn't care less	Neither do I	How's it going?	Good for you
I take your point	If I were you	I'm just looking	You never know
You may as well	Most of all	I need a hand	Guess what?
Someone or other	Even so	For a start	It's early days
The sooner the better	Now and then	Just the thing	I'll tell you what
Wish you were here	Who'd have thought?	On my own	At the end of the day

✂

2.11 Body talk

Memory focus	Making spoken utterances memorable by linking them to physical gestures.
Level	Pre-intermediate and above
Time	15 minutes plus
Preparation	Choose a list of about 20 spoken utterances appropriate for your group or make copies of the list in Box 2.11.

Procedure

1 Elicit possible contexts in which a few of the utterances in Box 2.11 might be said. Now ask the learners to go through the utterances in pairs, deciding on a brief context for each one. Which ones do they already feel able to use themselves in natural speech? Which ones would they like to be able to use more naturally?

2 Ask each learner to choose three of the utterances and to decide on a physical gesture to go with each one. They then practise repeating all three, with the appropriate gestures. It helps if the gestures are exaggerated as much as possible.

3 When you feel that they are ready, call out a number (1, 2 or 3). Simultaneously, the learners keep repeating the utterance with the gesture until another number is called. Change the number frequently so that learners are kept on their toes.

4 Ask everyone to stand up and find a partner. Choose one pair to work with to demonstrate the activity. Learner A in the pair says his or her first utterance, with the accompanying gesture, to Learner B. Learner B then replies with another utterance and gesture. They keep repeating their lines as if in a dialogue. Now ask all the pairs to do the same thing. Each pair needs to practise their exchange and make sure they make a mental note of the person they are working with before changing partners and repeating the process. They then do this again for their third utterances. Now when you call out a number, learners have to find the right partner and keep performing their dialogues (and the gestures that go with them) until you call out a different number.

5 Ask learners to come together in groups of three to five. Ask them to make a moving sculpture which incorporates each person's three utterances with accompanying gestures. When they have had a chance to decide on an order and to rehearse, these can then be presented to the rest of the class.

Box 2.11: Body talk

Where've you been?	What would you like?	Is this yours?
Could you give me a hand?	Hurry up, please!	Watch out!
Could you say that again?	I don't feel very well.	Can I have one?
What happened to you?	I'd better be going.	Help yourself.
Would you like a bite?	Ugh, that's horrible!	You're joking!
Which one do you want?	That's fantastic news!	Are you alright?
I don't agree with you.	What can I get you?	I don't really get it.
That tastes really nice.	Make yourself at home.	Take it easy.

From *Memory Activities for Language Learning*
© Cambridge University Press 2011   PHOTOCOPIABLE

Note

On a plane journey, I once sat next to a teacher of Portuguese sign language who was himself deaf. It was amazing how much he was able to teach me in sign language, in a short space of time, and how much we were able to communicate through this. It would seem that gestures are far more easily remembered than words. In this and the following activity, I exploit this fact by making clear links between gestures and the language they represent. Before doing these activities, however, it is important to be mindful of the cultural sensitivities of the learners in your class; gestures are not universal but connote different things in different cultures. It is possible that learners may find some gestures offensive.

2.12 Skeleton stories

Memory focus	Using physical activity to make the language of a story memorable. The examples used here focus particularly on the use of prepositions and past verb forms.
Level	Any (The example 'A walk in the forest' is for elementary level and above and the example 'The fisherman's nightmare' is for intermediate level and above.)
Time	10 minutes plus
Preparation	Choose a story that can be mimed fairly easily (see Box 2.12a for two examples). If using the variation, prepare a skeleton text of the story like the examples in Box 2.12c. In this case, each learner will need a copy of the skeleton text (preferably enlarged).

Procedure

1   Ask the class to stand up, in as much space as is possible.

2   Tell the learners that you are going to read out a short story to them and that they should act out each line as you read it.

3   Read out the story, pausing after each line to allow time for everyone to respond physically. It helps if they make their gestures as big as possible. Explain to the students that if they do not understand something, they should follow those who do. If no one understands a line, you will need to mime it yourself to make the meaning clear.

4   Repeat the story, but this time read at a faster pace.

5   Ask everyone to retell what they can remember of the story in pairs. While they do that, write the 'first letters only' version of the story on the board (see Box 2.12b). Now ask them to go through the story again, using the letters on the board as a memory aid. Finally, go through the complete story with everyone, by pointing to the letters on the board and asking the class to say the appropriate words.

6   One person in each pair now tells the story by looking at the board while the other learner performs it.

Variation

Instead of using first letters, learners can be given the complete text represented by a series of gaps (see Box 2.12c.). Tell them that each line represents one letter and the gaps represent the spaces between words. Working together in pairs or small groups, the learners fill in as much of the text as they can. If they get stuck, you can help by feeding in some of the words, or by reading the complete text again while they act it out. The task can be made simpler by including more completed words in the skeleton text you give them, or by including the first letter of some or all of the words. This version is based on 'Cheating with Mime' in *Dictation: New Methods, New Possibilities* by Paul Davis and Mario Rinvolucri, Cambridge University Press, 1988.

Note
While it is important not to frustrate learners by over-challenging them with the task, neither should things be made too easy! A lot of learning happens when learners try to recall how they moved in the story and when they discuss in pairs the different possibilities for each space.

Box 2.12a: Skeleton stories

A walk in the forest

I was walking in the forest.

I saw a box on the ground in front of me.

I picked it up.

I slowly opened the lid.

Aahh! A bird flew out and hit me in the face!

I looked inside.

Wow! It was full of treasure!

I filled up my pockets as quickly as I could.

Oh no! Someone was coming!

I turned around and ran.

 ----

continued

Box 2.12a: (*cont.*)

The fisherman's nightmare

I was walking along a beach.

Suddenly I stopped.

I looked down at the sand in front of me.

Wow! A piece of chocolate cake!

I bent down and picked it up.

I smelt it.

It smelt amazing!

I took a small bite.

It tasted fantastic.

I put the whole piece in my mouth.

Disaster!

I felt the hook in my mouth.

I was being pulled into the sea.

I held the line with both hands.

I pulled as hard as I could.

Then I remembered the knife in my pocket.

I took it out and cut the line.

I was free!

But I haven't been fishing since.

From *Memory Activities for Language Learning*

Box 2.12b: Skeleton stories

A walk in the forest

i w w i t f.

i s a b o t g i f o m.

i p i u.

i s o t l.

Aahh! a b f o a h m i t f!

i l i.

Wow! i w f o t!

i f u m p a q a i c.

Oh no! s w c!

i t a a r!

✂--

continued

Box 2.12b: (*cont.*)

The fisherman's nightmare

iwwaab.

sis.

ildatsifom.

Wow! apocc!

ibdapiu.

isi.

isa!

itasb.

itf!

iptwpimm.

d!

ifthimm.

iwbpits.

ihtlwbh.

ipahaic.

tirtkimp.

itioactl.

iwf!

bihbfs.

From *Memory Activities for Language Learning*
© Cambridge University Press 2011

Box 2.12c: Skeleton stories

A walk in the forest

_ ___ _____ __ ___ _____.

_ ___ _ ___ __ ___ _____ __ _____ __ __.

_ _____ __ __.

_ _____ _____ ___ ___.

Aahh! _ ____ ____ ___ ___ ___ __ __ ___ ____!

_ _____ _____.

Wow! __ ___ ____ __ _____!

_ _____ __ __ _____ __ _____ __ _ _____.

Oh, no! _____ ___ _____!

_ _____ _____ ___ ___.

✂---

continued

Box 2.12c: (*cont.*)

The fisherman's nightmare

– ––– –––––– ––––– – –––––.

–––––––– – –––––––.

– –––––– –––– –– ––– –––– –– ––––– –– ––.

Wow! – ––––– –– –––––––– ––––!

– –––– –––– ––– –––––– –– ––.

– ––––– ––.

–– ––––– –––––––!

– –––– – ––––– ––––.

–– –––––– –––––––––!

– ––– ––– –––––– ––––– –– –– –––––.

––––––––!

– –––– ––– –––– –– –– –––––.

– ––– ––––– –––––– –––– ––– –––.

– –––– ––– –––– –––– –––– –––––.

– –––––– –– –––– –– – –––––.

–––– – –––––––––– ––– ––––– –– –– ––––––.

– –––– –– ––– ––– ––– ––– ––––.

– ––– –––!

                  ,
––– – –––––– –––– ––––––– –––––.

From *Memory Activities for Language Learning*
© Cambridge University Press 2011   PHOTOCOPIABLE

Follow-up

Learners prepare their own skeleton story texts for homework. These are handed in for checking and used with their classmates in another class.

2.13 Treasure hunt

Memory focus	Making vocabulary memorable through movement, competition and linking it to a particular place.
Level	Any
Time	10 minutes plus
Preparation	Write a list of about 20 words or chunks which belong to two distinct categories. (See Box 2.13 for examples for beginner and upper intermediate learners.) Now write each word on a small sticky label. Mix them up and stick them around the classroom in places where they will not easily be seen by the learners, e.g. on the underside of chairs or tables, behind pictures on the walls, under rugs or carpets on the floor, on the ceiling. Make sure that some are fairly easy to spot and others are much more difficult. If an outside space is available, there may be a more interesting range of hiding places to choose from.

Procedure

1 Organize the class into pairs. Tell them what the two categories are. Each pair needs a sheet of paper with the two categories written on it. This sheet must remain at their desks. The pairs need to go around the room looking for words. When they find something, they should try to agree on which category it belongs to, go back to their desks and write it under the appropriate heading. The trick is to do all this without letting other pairs know where the words are.

2 When one pair has found all 20 words, or after a set amount of time, ask everyone to write their names on their sheets and swap with another pair. Go through the answers with the whole class, checking meanings as you go. They get a point for each word in the right category but lose a point for a word written in the wrong category. Each pair marks the sheet they have in front of them. The pair with the most points at the end wins.

Follow-up
Go through some of the locations and see if learners can remember which language item was located there. They can often do this surprisingly well. After a few examples, this can be turned into a pair-work activity.

Box 2.13: Treasure hunt

Beginners

Food and drink

cake, bread, fish, meat, apples, biscuits, coffee, potatoes, wine, butter, chips, peas

Clothes

hat, jumper, trousers, shoes, jacket, coat, socks, tie

Upper intermediate

let

... go of my arm, ... sleeping dogs lie, ... your hair down,
... off steam, ... the cat out of the bag, ... him off the hook,
... me into the bathroom, ... me see, ...'s face it

keep

... up the good work, ... away from me!, ... saying the same thing,
... off the grass, ... to the path, ... your fingers crossed,
... your eyes peeled, ... an eye on things, ... up with all the housework,
... still!, ... making the same mistakes

From *Memory Activities for Language Learning*
© Cambridge University Press 2011   PHOTOCOPIABLE

2.14 Silly grammar

Memory focus	Making tenses memorable by challenging learners to create silly examples.
Level	Elementary and above
Time	20 minutes
Preparation	Choose the tense to be practised and plan a substitution table framework for it. See the example below for the past continuous tense.

Procedure

1 If working with the past continuous tense, draw a table like the one below on the board.

1	2	3	4	5	6	7
	frying		umbrella		teacher	spoke

2 Now elicit from the class about 10 words which belong to the same word class as the examples in squares 2, 4, 6 and 7. Write the words in the appropriate square as they say them. Emphasize that there does not need to be any meaning relationship between the words, they should just fit into the grammatical categories. These categories are:

2 = transitive verb+-*ing*; 4 = object; 6 = animal or person; 7 = past form of intransitive verb (verb 2 form).

3 Now add the missing words from the other tables yourself so that you end up with something like this.

1	2	3	4	5	6	7
While I	frying	a/an	umbrella	a/an	teacher	spoke
was	ironing	the	telephone	the	sister	flew
	cutting	my	house	my	doctor	exploded
	inviting	your	pencil	your	brother	cried
	pushing		computer		rabbit	laughed
	following		dustbin		tiger	smiled
	swallowing		window		monkey	died
	counting		brain		cow	smoked
	teaching		door		uncle	cooked
	washing		motorway		salmon	whistled

4   Ask learners to look at the table and to write down one or two of the silliest sentences they can come up with. Ask them to share these in small groups and then write some of them up on the board. Discuss with the class whether they think these kinds of examples make the grammar easier to remember than more standard ones (e.g. *While I was getting in the bath, the telephone rang; While I was watching television, the lights went out*, etc.).

Follow-up
Learners draw a picture of one of their sentences. These are then displayed around the room and other learners discuss which sentences they think they represent.

Note
Created examples of grammar, such as *The philosopher pulled the lower jaw of the hen*, recalled by Sweet (1899), have been criticized for being unnatural and unlike real English. Guy Cook (2000) has argued, however, that the very fact that such sentences are bizarre and unnatural may help to make the grammar embedded within them more memorable for learners.

3 Retrieving

No matter how effective the initial storage of a language item may have been, without regular opportunities for retrieval from memory, there is still a chance that it may be lost forever. A principal role of the language teacher then is to draw on, and draw out, what has gone before. New language needs to be regularly revisited in different, stimulating contexts, and ultimately needs to be used in meaningful ways in order for the learners to feel a sense of ownership of it.

The least demanding form of retrieval is receptive, whereby learners re-encounter the form of a word, for example, in a reading or listening text, and are challenged both to recognize it and to make sense of it. But simply reading or hearing a word again, being used in exactly the same way, may do little to extend its memorability. We could check understanding of the items by asking the learners to translate them, or to provide synonyms, but better still would be to encourage them to 'put the words to work' in some way. This could be by using them in speech or in writing, or by providing a description or definition from which others can guess the word. It will also be useful if new encounters enable the learners to discover something new. For instance, if they learn the word *frame* as a surrounding for a picture, to later discover one of its more figurative meanings, such as *to be framed for murder*, will create more associations within the mental lexicon and also provide a strong and memorable mental image.

Productive retrieval presents a still greater challenge to learners. Here they are provided with the meaning, or a situation which calls for the word, and are expected to retrieve the form. There may be difficult issues with pronunciation or spelling which deter learners from attempting to reproduce the word (for fear of consequently losing face), and on top of this, there is the pressure to produce language in real time, particularly when speaking.

As challenging as this may be, the evidence suggests that, providing it is successful and does not lead to frustration, productive retrieval is the most useful form for strengthening the links which are so beneficial in retaining language items in long-term memory. It seems that we are more likely to remember something if there has been an element of struggle involved in the process of retrieval. There is also a further complication, however: productive retrieval is far more difficult to set up and control by the teacher. How can we ensure that learners will produce the language that we want them to and not fall back on safer alternatives?

Perhaps a happy medium is to engage learners in activities that require both receptive and productive retrieval at the same time. Many of the activities in this chapter involve only some of the learners seeing the form of a language item. The teacher then has to make those who cannot see it produce it – perhaps by explaining the words or providing some other form of prompt. As long as these roles are swapped around regularly, everyone will be engaged with both receptive and productive retrieval at some stage in the lesson.

Another important issue to consider is how frequently, and to what extent, retrieval activities are needed. Most researchers agree that little and often are the key, and that retrieval activities may decrease in frequency as more time passes from the original encounter. They also suggest that the optimal moment for retrieving a language item is when it is on the verge of being forgotten. Of course, the more words a learner has stored, the more unlikely it is that everything will be retrieved through natural exposure and use alone, and the greater the need for activities which target specific areas. In practical terms, spending a few minutes in each class reactivating what has just been learnt, as well as regularly spending time going back to areas of language that are less readily accessible, may be the most suitable approach to take.

With different learners requiring varying degrees of retrieval for a particular area of language, the process also becomes more difficult to manage by the teacher. Ideally, learners gradually need to start taking responsibility for managing this retrieval process themselves. The evidence also suggests that this is another factor in helping to increase the memorability of the language being retrieved. An additional purpose of the classroom activities described here, then, is that they can serve as useful models for independent learning elsewhere.

Using a word bag

Reviewing language that has previously been focused on does not need to take up a lot of class time and can also serve the purpose of providing a change of pace and energizing the group. Having a class 'word bag' is a great way of making sure that this 'old' language is regularly being recycled and reactivated in motivating and useful ways. The basic procedure is that whenever a new word or chunk of language comes up in class, it is written on a small piece of paper and put inside the bag. This could be done by the teacher, or alternatively, different learners can be assigned the role of adding to it, by copying language from the board or from their coursebook at the end of each lesson.

As a regular feature of the classes, learners can then pick up to 10 of the pieces of paper each and work with them in pairs or small groups. Here are some short and snappy activities that can be done.

- *Decision making*: Learners go through the words they have picked and sort them into at least three different categories of their choosing. They then explain their choice of categories to the others in their group. One interesting way of doing this is to view the language items as something they would put in their fridge, their freezer or their dustbin.
  - Fridge: I'll be able to use these language items in my day-to-day life.
  - Freezer: I don't need to use these language items now, but I'll save them for when I do.
  - Dustbin: I don't think I'll ever need to use these language items.
- *Creating a context*: Learners work in pairs with about 10 language items. They write a dialogue or a very short story which uses all of the items they have picked. These are then performed or read out to the others. The pairs who are listening can be asked to guess which words the speakers were challenged to use.
- *Creating a test*: Learners create a wordsearch, a crossword or another type of puzzle where the words to be reviewed are the answers. This can be done with pen and paper or online at a website such as http:// puzzlemaker.discoveryeducation.com/ Learners then try to find the answers to each other's puzzles.

Guessing games
- Learners mime their words to each other.
- One person says a sentence which might contain the language item, but replaces it with the sound 'buzz'. For example:
  - A: I was very tired, so I buzz to bed early.
  - B: went
- Someone describes the meaning of the word to the others, without saying the language item itself. For example:
  - A: It's a way of saying very big.
  - B: massive
- Learner A writes the word with her finger on Learner B's back. Learner B has to guess the word.

- One learner just says the beginning of the item, and the others have to guess the complete item. This is good for raising awareness about the individual sounds that words contain. For example:

    A: /wɔː/
    B: water
    A: /wɔːd/
    B: wardrobe

3.1 Mime race

Memory focus	Helping learners to recall and reactivate words and chunks through mime.
Level	Any
Time	5–15 minutes
Preparation	The teacher (or a learner) prepares a list of vocabulary items to be reviewed. Each group of learners needs a set of these which have been cut up into individual items.

Procedure

1 The learners work in groups of three to seven. Each group gets a set of the slips of paper. They should spread them out face down on a chair or table.
2 The learners take it in turns to mime one of the words or chunks to the other members of their group. When they have guessed what it says, a different person takes a word and mimes it. Each group works simultaneously and as quickly as possible. The group that guesses the most words in 10 minutes is the winner.

Note

Engaging in mime races in small groups is a very effective way of reactivating a wide range of language items in a short space of time. Though this activity is easier with concrete areas of vocabulary, such as objects, jobs and actions, it can also be used with more abstract words. It is worth noting that the more difficult the word is to mime, the more language is usually produced by those who are watching.

Variation

Instead of miming the words, the learners take turns to draw them for each other (again without speaking) or describe the word in some way so that the other person can guess it.

3.2 Word cards

Memory focus	Challenging retrieval of vocabulary and/or grammar.
Level	Any
Time	5–15 minutes
Preparation	At the end of a lesson, make a note of the language which has been put on the board and bring it to the next class. See Box 3.2a for an example from a beginners' group. Cut up enough slips of paper so that each pair or small group can write one of the language items on each slip.

Procedure

1 Rewrite the language items on the board, or project them using a prepared slide. Give out a set of the cut-up slips of paper to each pair or small group. (If working in a multilingual classroom, it may be helpful to group together learners who speak the same mother tongue – L1.) Ask them to write one of the language items on each slip. This should ideally be written in pencil, rather than ink, so that it does not show through.

2 Now ask them to turn over the slips and write an L1 translation on the reverse of each one. They may need to use dictionaries or consult you for assistance.

3 Ask them to go through the complete set with the English version facing upwards. They should say the L1 version and then turn the slip over to check.

4 They now turn the papers the other way up. Looking at the L1 version, they try to remember the English version, before turning over to see if they are right. They keep going through all of the slips until they can remember them all.

5 Learners may take the cards away with them for self-study, or they can be added to the class word bag for reuse in future classes.

Note

The use of word cards has been popularized by Paul Nation. You can read about research into their effectiveness in *Learning Vocabulary in Another Language* by I.S.P. Nation, Cambridge University Press, 2001. See also http://quizlet.com, a website which allows teachers and learners to create word cards, and to use those that have already been created by others.

Variation

1   Give each group a ready-made set of cards to work with. Apart from translation, this procedure lends itself to a variety of different ways of manipulating language. One form can be written on one side of the card and the other form on the other.

   - present verb form / past verb form (*I go shopping every day / I went shopping yesterday*, etc.)
   - adjective form / noun form (*She's really strong / She has a lot of strength*, etc.)
   - question and answer (*Where do you live? / In Paris*, etc.)
   - phrasal verb / non-phrasal verb (*She puts up with the noise / She tolerates the noise*, etc.)

2   Ask learners to draw pictures on the reverse of the cards to represent the word or sentence. The pictures in Box 3.2b were drawn by learners to show the following present perfect sentences: *He's eaten too much, She's lost her keys, He's broken his arm, They've just had an argument.*

3   Groups can prepare sets of cards focusing on different areas of language for other groups to use.

Box 3.2a: Word cards

We need the light on.	I went to Libya last month.
I'm dirty. I need a shower.	I need to buy a new coat.
I went to the pub on Saturday.	I need help from my teacher.
I went to Plymouth on Sunday.	There's a picture on the wall.
I went to my parents' house on Friday.	I need to eat something.

Box 3.2b: Word cards

From *Memory Activities for Language Learning*
© Cambridge University Press 2011

3.3 Vocabulary race

Memory focus	Challenging learners to quickly recall words belonging to particular lexical sets.
Level	Any
Time	5–10 minutes
Preparation	Choose a lexical set to review for every 10 learners in the class. In addition to lexical sets (food, drinks, the weather, clothes, nationalities, etc.), you could use sets with a grammar focus (e.g. past verb forms, positive adjectives to describe people, verbs that are followed by -*ing* forms, etc.) or with collocations (e.g. expressions using *get/have/take*, etc.).

Procedure

1 Divide the class into groups of up to 10 students. Divide the board up vertically into 2, 3 or 4 sections depending on the number of students. Write each of the category titles at the top of each section.

2 Now explain the rules of the game. Each group has to list as many words as possible to fit their category in a set amount of time (say three minutes). They do this by individually running up to the board, writing a word, and then running back and passing the board pen to the next person in their team. Those who are not running up to the board must stand behind a line (as far away from the board as space will allow). If anyone gets stuck, the other members of the team can make suggestions – but only when the person is behind the line.

3 After a set amount of time, or when you feel they have exhausted their ideas, call the activity to a halt. Go through all the items on the board together, awarding one point for each item in the correct category, and two points if it is also spelt correctly.

3.4 Jumbled chunk race

Memory focus	Retrieval of language items focused on in a previous class. Encouraging learners to store lexical chunks as single units.
Level	Any
Time	5–15 minutes
Preparation	You need to prepare some jumbled-up sentences using an area of language that has previously been focused on. Each sentence needs to be written on a large piece of paper, or if using PowerPoint® software, on an individual slide. See Box 3.4 for some examples using collocations and set phrases with *take*.

Procedure

1 Divide the class into groups of up to six learners. Ask each group to choose a name for their team and write these on the board.
2 Now explain the rules of the game.
  - a) You are going to display a jumbled-up sentence on the projector, or on a large piece of paper.
  - b) Everyone should try to work out as quickly as they can what the correct order of the sentence is.
  - c) When someone thinks they know what it is, they shout out the name of their team.
  - d) Whichever team is first has the chance to say what they think the sentence should be.
  - e) If they are correct, their team is awarded two points. If not, all the other teams are awarded one point and the next team to shout out their name has a chance to guess.
3 Display the sentences one by one. The team with the most points at the end is the winner.

Follow-up
This game can be used regularly at the beginning of class as a way of reviewing language. Learners can also be asked to take responsibility for preparing the jumbled sentences.

Box 3.4: Jumbled chunk race

1 time up takes too it much
   It takes up too much time.

✂ -

2 take don't to it heart
   Don't take it to heart.

✂ -

3 she shop to it to the back take had
   She had to take it back to the shop.

✂ -

4 dad really he after takes his
   He really takes after his dad.

✂ -

5 my been over taken by job's else someone
   My job's been taken over by someone else.

✂ -

6 four years every place the take Olympics
   The Olympics take place every four years.

✂ -

7 people are how taking many part?
   How many people are taking part?

✂ -

8 surprise really me took it by
   It really took me by surprise.

✂ -

9 you'll to my for it have take word
   You'll have to take my word for it.

✂ -

10 I windsurfing know lots of who've up taken people
   I know lots of people who've taken up windsurfing

From *Memory Activities for Language Learning*
© Cambridge University Press 2011   PHOTOCOPIABLE

3.5 Guess our chunks

Memory focus	Challenging retrieval of a range of lexical chunks related to key verbs.
Level	Intermediate and above (but see variation for lower-level versions)
Time	20 minutes plus
Preparation	Choose one key verb and write out five chunks which start with it (and which you think the class will know) on a piece of paper. For example for *get*, the list could be *get married, get upset, get up, get home* and *get to work*. Also think of some other key verbs which the class should know some collocations for and write each one on a small slip of paper (e.g. *make, do, take, have, keep, let*, etc.).

Procedure

1 To demonstrate the activity, tell the class that you have written five collocations with *get* on your piece of paper. Give an example to make sure they understand (e.g. *get lost*) and then tell them that they have one minute to guess what the five things that you have written are. Confirm each correct guess that they shout out by writing it up on the board as they say it. Stop after a minute and reveal the ones that they did not guess. Make sure everyone is clear about what each chunk means and how it is used in a sentence by establishing examples.

2 Now give each group of three to five learners one of the key words. Ask them to write a list of exactly five chunks which include the word. They should set each chunk within a sentence so that meanings are clear. If a group finishes quickly, give them an extra one to do. Go round the class and check that what they are writing is accurate.

3 When all the groups have done at least one verb, the activity works as in the demonstration. Each group says what the name of the verb is. The others have one minute to try to guess what the five chunks that they have written down are. Write any guesses that are confirmed as correct on the board. At the end of the minute, check understanding by eliciting example sentences where necessary.

4 The team with the greatest number of chunks that were not guessed is the winner.

Note

This activity challenges learners to retrieve language in two ways. First, in a measured and controlled way by planning their sentences in groups. Here they may receive support from each other as well as the teacher. Secondly, language may be retrieved as part of a more spontaneous and independent activity, where learners have the opportunity to shout out guesses. With large groups this stage can be rather noisy. It may be more appropriate therefore to allow only one group to guess at a time.

Variation
This activity can also be used to review many other areas of language, some of which are suited to much lower levels. These could be vocabulary-based (e.g. food, drink, animals, clothes, jobs, things you find in a kitchen/living room/bedroom, things made of wood/glass/metal, means of transport, etc.) or grammar-based (e.g. irregular past verb forms, positive/negative adjectives to describe people, verbs that are followed by -ing forms, adverbs of manner, etc.).

3.6 Hot seat

Memory focus	Retrieving language that has previously been focused on through contextualization and verbalization.
Level	Elementary and above
Time	5–10 minutes
Preparation	Prepare a list of language items (single words or chunks) to be reviewed, or ask a learner to do this.

Procedure
1 Divide the class into two sides. Choose one learner from each side to come to the front of the class and ask them to face away from the board.
2 Write a word or chunk on the board from your list. The rest of the learners now have to try to make the person at the front from their side say exactly what is written on the board. They do this by describing the word or by giving an example sentence (without mentioning the word itself, of course).
3 Whoever says the language item first gets a point for their side, and then two different people come to the front and the game continues.

Variation
With a large class, this activity can also be done in smaller groups, where each group is given a complete set of the items to be reviewed on separate pieces of paper.

3.7 I reckon they'll know that

Memory focus	Encouraging learners to reflect on cloze tests that have already been done and assess whether improvements have occurred.
Level	Pre-intermediate and above
Time	10 minutes plus
Preparation	You will need copies of two different cloze tests (texts where a certain number of words have been replaced by blanks) that have previously been done by the learners, plus the answer sheets that go with them.

Procedure

1   Divide the class into groups of four or five. Each group is divided into two pairs, or a pair and a three. Where possible, pair weaker and stronger learners together.

2   Each pair gets a copy of the cloze test (a different one from the other pair in their group) plus the answer sheet that goes with it. They then go through the text, discussing each gap and deciding which ones they think the other pair will get right and which they think they will get wrong, and marking this on the sheet.

3   Each pair then gets a clean copy of the other pair's cloze test. They go through it, try to agree on an answer for each gap and write it in. When they have finished, they swap sheets with the other pair, who mark their answers.

4   Groups now come together to discuss which questions they predicted would be answered correctly and which ones actually were. A competitive element can be introduced by awarding pairs a point for each correct prediction.

Variation

Rewrite a cloze text that the learners have already done so that there are no longer any gaps in it. Ask the learners to underline all the words that they think were represented as gaps when they did the test. Then, in groups, they can compare the words they have underlined and discuss why they think each gap was chosen. Finally give out the original cloze test for them to compare with their versions.

3.8 Gap-filling second time around

Memory focus	Encouraging learners to go back to gap-fill exercises they have already done and to notice improvements.
Level	Any
Time	5–10 minutes (the activity can be repeated over several classes)
Preparation	Make a copy of any sentence-level gap-fill or sentence-transformation type exercises from the coursebook that the learners have done. You can also create your own exercises to test areas of language that have been focused on in class. Each sentence should be put on an individual piece of card with the correct answer written on the back. See Box 3.8 for an example.

Procedure

1 Divide the learners into small groups. Give each group a set of the cards. They place them on the table in a pile, question side up.
2 As a group they go through all of the questions, trying to remember what the answer is before turning over to check.
3 Groups who finish quickly may receive a new set or swap them with another group.
4 The questions can be added to and recycled in later classes.

Box 3.8: Gap-filling second time around

On one side ...	On the other side ...
The film was dubbed. I prefer .... so you can hear the original language.	*subtitles*
When did the rain start? (*been*)	*How long has it been raining?*

Note
Encouraging learners to revisit exercises that they have already done can help to show them any improvements that have been made and raise awareness about where any gaps in their knowledge might be.

Variations
For an extra challenge, learners take it in turns to pick a card from the pack and read out the question without showing it to the others. As they read, they

replace each gap by saying 'buzz' instead, and the others have to say what 'buzz' represents. This takes the activity to another level because it requires accurate pronunciation and listening skills. If you have enough cards, the activity can also be done on an individual basis, with learners swapping cards with each other as they finish.

3.9 First-letter verb phrases

Memory focus	Retrieving verb phrases through first-letter hints.
Level	Any
Time	5 minutes plus
Preparation	Write out a sequence of events using verb phrases suitable for the level of the class. After each verb phrase, show how it can be reduced to first-letter hints, and then replace it by these hints in the next line. Each line should be written on a separate PowerPoint® slide or, if using an overhead projector, on a separate line. See the example for a beginners' class in Box 3.9.

Procedure

1   Show only the first line, using the projector. Check that everyone understands the meanings using mime, translation or concept checking. Establish that the 'WU' in Box 3.9 stands for *woke up*.

2   Show only the second line. Ask someone to read the line, replacing the letters by the words they represent. Again check understanding of the new verb phrase.

3   Keep repeating this process all the way through the sentences. At the end, ask learners in pairs to try to recall all of the verb phrases without looking at the hints.

Follow-up

Ask learners to write their own sequences of events in the same format as in Box 3.9. This could be about what they did at the weekend or whilst on holiday, for example. After being checked for accuracy, these can then be used in class by the learners in the same way that they were used by the teacher.

Box 3.9: First-letter verb phrases

He **woke up** (WU).

✂--

He WU and **got out of bed** (GOOB).

✂--

He WU, GOOB and **went to the bathroom** (WTTB).

✂--

He WU, GOOB, WTTB and then **brushed his teeth** (BHT).

✂--

He WU, GOOB, WTTB, BHT and then **had a shower** (HAS).

✂--

He WU, GOOB, WTTB, BHT, HAS and then **got dressed** (GD).

✂--

He WU, GOOB, WTTB, BHT, HAS, GD and then **had breakfast** (HB).

✂--

He WU, GOOB, WTTB, BHT, HAS, GD, HB and then **put on his shoes and coat** (POHSAC).

✂--

He WU, GOOB, WTTB, BHT, HAS, GD, HB, POHSAC and then **left the house** (LTH).

✂--

He WU, GOOB, WTTB, BHT, HAS, GD, HB, POHSAC, LTH and then **got on the bus** (GOTB).

✂--

He WU, GOOB, WTTB, BHT, HAS, GD, HB, POHSAC, LTH and GOTB.

From *Memory Activities for Language Learning*
© Cambridge University Press 2011   PHOTOCOPIABLE

3.10 Guess the text

Memory focus	Challenging learners to retrieve the language of a text.
Level	Any
Time	15 minutes plus
Preparation	Choose or write a dialogue or short text appropriate to the level of the class (Box 3.10a) and write it on the board with a line representing each word of the text.

Procedure

1 Invite one learner to the front of the class and engage in a role-play activity with him or her that explores the same situation as the dialogue you will be using. Try to use as much language from the dialogue as possible.

2 Everyone now tries out the role play in pairs. Ask them to swap roles around halfway through.

3 Now divide the class into up to four teams. Direct their attention to the gapped dialogue on the board (Box 3.10b).

4 Tell them that it represents a dialogue in a clothes shop. Each line represents one word and their task is to guess what the words are. Allow each group some time to brainstorm which words they think may be in the dialogue.

5 Now explain how the game works. Each team has the chance to guess a word that they think is in the dialogue. If they are correct, you write in all the examples of the word in the text and they have another go. If they are incorrect, the play passes to the next team. The team that guesses the last word of the dialogue is the winner.

Tip: The activity can be made easier by providing some of the words either before starting the task or when it is under way. In the dialogue below, the words *T-shirts, boyfriend* and *one's* are usually the most difficult words to guess.

Box 3.10a: Guess the text

A: Hi. Can I help you?
B: Yeah. How much are these T-shirts?
A: They're £19.99. Is it for you?
B: No, it's for my boyfriend.
A: What size is he?
B: Medium, I think.
A: This one's a medium.
B: Thanks very much.

From *Memory Activities for Language Learning*
© Cambridge University Press 2011   PHOTOCOPIABLE

Box 3.10b: Guess the text

A: _____. _____ _____ _____ _____?

B: _____. _____ _____ _____ _____ _____?

A: _____ £19.99. _____ _____ _____ _____?

B: _____, _____ _____ _____ _____.

A: _____ _____ _____ _____?

B: _____, _____ _____.

A: _____ _____ _____ _____.

B: _____ _____ _____.

From *Memory Activities for Language Learning*
© Cambridge University Press 2011   PHOTOCOPIABLE

Variation
This activity can be done using a storyboard software system. All the examples of a guessed word are then automatically filled into the text, making the activity easier to manage for the teacher.

3.11 Languaging memories 1: the first time

Memory focus	Using questions as a stimulus to retrieve, discuss and write about memories.
Level	Pre-intermediate and above
Time	30 minutes plus
Preparation	Make a copy of the questions in Box 3.11 for each learner, or display them on a projector.

Procedure

1   Show the questions to the learners. Allow them plenty of time to read the questions and think about how they might be able to answer them.
2   Now ask them each to choose six questions that they would feel comfortable answering and can provide interesting answers to. They should mark these questions with a tick.
3   Learners now swap sheets with a partner. They interview each other using the questions that have been chosen.
4   Learners write up what they can remember of the interview with their partners as a short text.
5   When they have finished, ask them to read each other's texts and comment on how accurately the information was remembered.

Box 3.11: Languaging memories 1: the first time

1 What can you remember about your first day at school?

2 What is your earliest memory?

3 Can you remember a difficult decision you've had to make in your life? What happened?

4 Are there any smells which remind you of a time long ago? What are they?

5 Can you remember your first ever English class? What was it like?

6 Can you remember when you learnt how to ride a bike/swim/drive? How was the experience?

7 Do you remember a really nice meal that you've had? Can you describe it?

8 Who was your first girlfriend/boyfriend? What do you remember about him/her?

9 What kind of games did you used to play when you were a small child?

10 Can you remember being told off at school? What did you do?

11 What's the best present you've ever been given?

12 Do you remember where you were on September 11th 2001?

13 Is there an event in your life that you remember very vividly? What is it?

14 Do you remember a really embarrassing moment in your life? What happened?

15 Can you remember a moment when you felt very proud?

From *Memory Activities for Language Learning*
© Cambridge University Press 2011   PHOTOCOPIABLE

Note

Most of the other activities in this book look at ways of helping learners to remember areas of language. But the retrieval of past memories is often also a motivating topic to talk about and one which can provide a useful challenge to learners' productive skills. This activity and Activity 3.12 work along these lines.

3.12 Languaging memories 2: smellyvision

Memory focus	Using smells as a stimulus to retrieve and talk about memories.
Level	Elementary and above
Time	20 minutes plus
Preparation	You will need a range of substances for smelling, one for each three or four learners. Some things to use could include cinnamon, mud, freshly cut grass, aniseed, marzipan, vinegar, beer, wine, cheese, perfume, aftershave, calamine lotion, basil, etc. Each substance needs to be put in a jar and ideally covered with tissue so it cannot be seen.

Procedure

1 Divide the class into small groups. Each group goes to one of the jars. They take off the lid and each person has a sniff of the contents. Everyone should say what the smell reminds them of. This could be a place, a time, a particular group of people, etc. They should give as much detail as possible of the memories that the smell evokes.

2 When they have finished, they move on to a different jar. Keep going until each group has visited every jar.

3 Each person chooses one of the smells that they experienced and writes a short paragraph about what the smell reminds them of (without mentioning the material itself).

4 Ask some people to read out their descriptions. Can the others in the class work out which of the materials it is that they are smelling? Alternatively, the teacher takes in the descriptions and reads them out loud for the class, reformulating inaccuracies or improving the texts in other ways as he or she goes. Now the class can guess which person they think wrote the description.

Note

Smelling something again can often take us back to our first encounter with it and can stir up strong feelings. Research has shown that there is a very powerful link between smells and emotional memory. It has even been suggested that our abilities to experience emotion at all developed out of our sense of smell.

4   Repeating and reactivating

As has been seen in the first three chapters of this book, there
is much that we can do as teachers to help learners with the process of
remembering new language, such as encouraging plenty of working-
memory processing of language, emphasizing memorability in the classroom
activities we choose, and incorporating retrieval activities regularly. But this
focus on memory applies not only to the way language is processed at a word
or sentence level, but also to the processing of complete texts and any work
that is done on skills development in the classroom.

So how can reading and listening texts be best exploited to maximize the
learners' ability to remember their contents? Clearly the more motivating the
material that the learners are exposed to, the greater the chances that they
will notice and remember things about it. At the same time, if learners are
encouraged to establish a link between exposure and use, by activating as
far as possible the language contained in the texts that they encounter, then
language is again more likely to become more memorable. In order for this
to happen, the gap in level between what learners are reading and listening to
and what they can produce themselves should not be too large.

Promoting language activation of texts could be as simple as asking
learners to discuss immediately, in pairs or small groups, what they have read
or heard, before its contents disappear from working memory completely.
But it can also be about the way in which we structure text-based lessons.
One reason for using texts at all in the classroom is to practise and develop
the skills involved in reading and listening in a second language, but this
is not always an area that is given high priority by the learners themselves.
Instead, they may principally see a focus on texts either as an opportunity
to notice and consequently remember more language, or as models for their
own speaking and writing. Many of the activities in this chapter explore
some practical ways of enabling learners to do both of these things.

Another area addressed by this chapter concerns revisiting texts that the
learners have already encountered. Sometimes the spoken and written texts
that learners are exposed to in coursebooks or other sources are encountered
only once, and for meaning-driven activities only. This is unlikely to help
learners much in remembering the language models they contain. By asking
learners to go back to these texts with different or more challenging tasks,

we can promote deeper processing of the language they contain through re-examination and noticing.

The need for repeating and recycling can also apply to the spoken and written texts that the learners have produced themselves. Research suggests that asking learners to redo speaking and writing tasks can lead to improvements in both accuracy and fluency. Each time they repeat a task, learners are able to devote more and more attention to the form of what they are saying, and consequently improvements may be made. If other learners, or the teacher, are also able to interact in some way with what is produced, then this can also encourage greater reflection and improved performance. Ultimately, this kind of task repetition may also lead to automatization of some of the language areas being used. The activities towards the end of this chapter suggest some motivating ways of incorporating repetition of output in the classroom.

Michalis's story

Michalis, a 24-year-old native speaker of Greek, spent five months of 1999 living in a small village in mountainous Sardinia. He arrived as a complete beginner, but within two to three months was speaking Italian fluently. By the end of his stay, he was able to produce quite complex spoken and written texts and was later assessed as being at B2 level in the Common European Framework of reference for languages.

Without attending classes, and with no formal structured learning involved whatsoever, how was this possible? Although many of the linguistic features of Italian were clearly being remembered in order for progress to happen so quickly, Michalis states that there was no conscious effort on his part to remember anything at all.

Michalis attributes much of his success to the opportunities for repetition which were given to him, and which he found for himself. During the time he was there, he interacted with a vast number of different people in the village and found that he was very quickly imitating the spoken language that he heard. This applied not just to the words themselves but also to the intonation patterns and any gestures which accompanied certain expressions. In fact, the more that these paralinguistic features were present, the easier he found it to recall and repeat the utterances.

Words and phrases that seemed to stick in his mind particularly were those which he couldn't make fit with what he already knew about the language. He recalls the 'Eureka' moments he felt when, after hearing such a phrase being used by many different speakers in so many different ways, he was finally able to unravel a complex linguistic riddle and understand something more about how the language worked.

Repetition also played its part in his own output. Whenever he met new people, he was often called upon to provide a spoken introductory text about himself. In the initial stages at least, this self-narrative was carefully planned and mentally rehearsed before performance. The same basic text was repeated with each new encounter, evolving as different listeners had the chance to interact with it, and becoming increasingly spontaneous and complex as his competence in the language developed.

4.1 The tie shop joke

Memory focus	Providing follow-up listening activities which challenge learners to recycle language.
Level	Any (the example text is for elementary level)
Time	25 minutes
Preparation	Each pair or small group needs a copy of the picture story in Box 4.1a and the story summary in Box 4.1b, which have been cut up into individual pieces.

Procedure

1   Give each pair or small group one set of the pictures. Ask them to put the pictures in order to make a coherent story.
2   Tell the story to the class, using mime and gestures to illustrate meanings where necessary.
3   After checking that everyone has got the right order, give out copies of the cut-up story summary. Again, ask the pairs to put these in order.
4   Read through the sentences in the correct order so that everyone can check their work.

Follow-up

1   Write a list of words and phrases in the mother tongue on the board and ask learners to find their equivalents in the English version of the story summary.
2   Put the learners into small groups and ask them to prepare a dramatized version of the story. Alternatively, ask them to prepare a performance using the scripted version of the story (Box 4.1c).

Box 4.1a: The tie shop joke

From *Memory Activities for Language Learning*
© Cambridge University Press 2011   PHOTOCOPIABLE

Box 4.1b: The tie shop joke

b) A man was driving his car in the desert. It was a hot day and he didn't have any water.

✂---

f) Suddenly his car stopped working. He tried to fix it, but he couldn't do anything. It was completely broken.

✂---

c) He walked and he walked and he walked. He was quite tired and quite thirsty.

✂---

h) Suddenly he came to a shop. 'Do you have any water?' he asked the shopkeeper. 'No,' said the shopkeeper, 'I only have ties.'

✂---

a) He walked and he walked and he walked. He was very tired and very thirsty.

✂---

d) Suddenly he came to a shop. 'Do you have any water?' he asked the shopkeeper. 'No,' said the shopkeeper, 'I only have ties.'

✂---

e) He walked and he walked and he walked. He was extremely tired and extremely thirsty.

✂---

g) Suddenly he came to a really nice restaurant. 'Do you have any water?' he asked the waiter. 'Yes, we do,' said the waiter. 'But I'm sorry, you can't come in. You don't have a tie on!'

From *Memory Activities for Language Learning*

Box 4.1c: The tie shop joke

Characters: Narrator 1, Narrator 2, Man, Shopkeeper 1, Shopkeeper 2, Waiter

(For smaller groups the two narrators could be played by the same person, as could the shopkeepers and waiter.)

Narrator 1:	There was once a man who was driving in the desert. It was a hot day and he was thirsty and tired.
Narrator 2:	Suddenly his car stopped working. He got out to try to fix it. But he couldn't do anything. It was completely broken.
Narrator 2:	It was a hot day and he was thirsty, but he didn't have any water.
Narrator 1:	And it was a very long way to the next town. He decided to walk.
Narrator 2:	He walked and he walked and he walked. He was tired and he was thirsty.
Narrator 1:	Suddenly he saw a shop in front of him. He was very happy and he ran to the shop.
Man:	Do you have any water?
Narrator 2:	… he said to the shopkeeper.
Shopkeeper 1:	No, I don't. But I do have lots of ties. I have long ties and short ties, and red ties and blue ties, and wide ties and narrow ties. All of my ties are very cheap. Do you want to buy one?
Man:	No, I don't. I'm very thirsty! Do you have just a little bit of water?
Shopkeeper 1:	I'm sorry. I don't.
Narrator 1:	So the man said goodbye and started to walk again. He walked and he walked and he walked. He was very tired, and very thirsty.
Narrator 2:	Suddenly he saw another shop in front of him. Again he was very happy and he ran to the shop.
Man:	Do you have any water?
Narrator 1:	… he said to the second shopkeeper.
Shopkeeper 2:	No, I don't. But I do have lots of ties. I have ties from Italy, ties from China, ties from England, ties from Brazil. I even have ties from Thailand! All of my ties are very cheap. Do you want to buy one?
Man:	No, I don't! I'm very thirsty! Do you have just a little tiny bit of water?
Shopkeeper 1:	I'm sorry. I don't.
Narrator 1:	So the man said goodbye and started to walk again. He walked and he walked and he walked. He was very, very tired, and very, very thirsty.
Narrator 2:	Suddenly he saw a beautiful restaurant in front of him. He was very, very happy. He ran to the restaurant.

continued

Box 4.1c: (*cont.*)

Man:	Do you have any water?
Narrator 1:	… he said to the waiter standing at the door.
Waiter:	Of course we do.
Man:	I'm very thirsty! Can I come in!
Waiter:	I'm sorry, sir. This is a very nice restaurant. You can't come in without a tie!

From *Memory Activities for Language Learning*
© Cambridge University Press 2011   PHOTOCOPIABLE

4.2 The three burglars magic trick

Memory focus	Challenging learners to remember the language of a listening text through structured activation.
Level	Pre-intermediate and above (for lower levels adapt the language level of the task and the way the story is told)
Time	30 minutes
Preparation	You will need a pack of playing cards for each small group of learners and copies of the task at Step 2 (or be prepared to project it, or write it on the board). You also need to familiarize yourself with the trick so that you can perform it smoothly (see Box 4.2b).

Procedure

1 Perform the trick to the class, adapting the level at which you speak to suit their needs. When you have finished, ask them if they know how it was done. If no one knows, reveal the secret to them.
2 Give out copies of a matching task such as the one in Box 4.2a (again adapted for the level), or project it or write it on the board. Ask learners to match a sentence stem from the left side with an ending from the right.
3 Check the answers with everyone. Now ask one learner in each pair to look at the task and test the other by saying the beginning of a sentence and getting their partner to complete it.
4 Organize the class into small groups and give each group a pack of playing cards. Ask them to try doing the magic trick on each other. Do they know any other magic tricks with a narrative element that they can show each other?

Box 4.2a: The three burglars magic trick

The burglars landed	some gold rings, diamond necklaces and expensive perfume.
The first burglar went to the kitchen and made	on the roof in their helicopter.
The second burglar went to the living room and took	on the roof to warn the others.
The third burglar went to the bedroom. He took	on the roof to keep watch.
The fourth burglar stayed	them all something to eat.
Suddenly he saw	on the roof and flew off in their helicopter.
He quickly banged	the television, the DVD player, the stereo and some paintings.
The other burglars all quickly got back	a policeman coming.

From *Memory Activities for Language Learning*
© Cambridge University Press 2011   PHOTOCOPIABLE

Box 4.2b: The three burglars magic trick

Preparation

Before you start the trick, get the cards ready. Find the four jacks and fan them out.

Take three additional cards from the pack and hide them from view behind the jacks.   *continued*

Box 4.2b: (*cont.*)

What you say	What you do
There were four burglars who had a very special way of stealing things from houses.	Show the four jacks fanned out. Don't show the three extra cards hidden behind.
What they did was to land on the roof in their helicopter.	Push all the jacks and the extra cards together and place them face down on the top of the pack.
The first burglar went down to the kitchen and made everybody something to eat. What did he find in the kitchen? (Elicit food items from the class and incorporate what they say into the story, e.g. bread, eggs, pasta, etc.)	Take the top card and place it inside the rest of the pack near the bottom. Don't show the learners what the card is. They will think it is a jack, but really it is one of the three hidden cards.
The second burglar went to the living room and started to steal what he could find. (Elicit ideas from the class again, e.g. TV, DVD player, stereo, paintings, etc.)	Take the next card from the top and place it in the middle of the pack (again without showing what the card is).
The third burglar went to the bedroom and started to steal what he found there. (Ask for more ideas from the class, e.g. gold rings, diamond necklaces, expensive perfume, etc.)	Take the next card and put it towards the top of the pack (without showing it).
The last burglar stayed at the top of the house to keep watch. He suddenly saw a police car coming down the road. He quickly banged on the roof and all of the burglars quickly got back on the roof and they flew off in their helicopter.	Show the four top cards, one by one, which will all be jacks!
	Fan out the rest of the pack to show that there aren't any extra jacks in it.

From *Memory Activities for Language Learning*
© Cambridge University Press 2011

Variation

Show the magic trick to only half the class, while the others are doing a different task. Then ask those who have seen the trick to perform it in small groups to those who have not. Alternatively, invite learners from different classes to come in and see it.

Note

One of the advantages of using 'live' as opposed to pre-recorded listening material is that it can be adapted to the level of the learners to make it more accessible as a model for learner output. After I had shown this magic trick to a group of beginners, one learner performed it to another low-level learner who had not seen the trick before. Although there were many differences between this performance (see transcript in Box 4.2c) and my original one, the learner was still challenged to activate some of the language from my telling and was entirely successful in his performance of the magic trick.

Box 4.2c: The three burglars magic trick

Learner 1: This four boys OK. This come and this upstairs OK. This go kitchen. Cooking and drink coffee and tea and cook. No problem.

Learner 2: No problem.

Learner 1: OK. This go bedroom.

Learner 2: Bathroom?

Learner 1: Bedroom. Because change clothes, sleep, revising. No problem?

Learner 2: No problem.

Learner 1: OK. This go living room because watch film action. This watch people. Come no come OK this people come no come. OK and car police come (makes police siren noise).

Learner 2: OK.

Learner 1: This boy 'Coming guys! Come on. Police coming. Come on guys'. This one, two, three, four (he reveals the four jacks at the top of the pack). OK.

Learner 2: OK!

4.3 Anecdotes

Memory focus	Providing opportunities for learners to notice the language used in a personal anecdote.
Level	Intermediate and above
Time	30 minutes plus
Preparation	Think of a couple of short personal anecdotes that you would feel comfortable telling your class and make a list of five or six chunks which are related to each. You also need some way of recording your speech, such as with a hand-held recording device.

Procedure

1 Write the key words and chunks which are related to your two anecdotes in a random order on the board. I used the following words when I did this activity with an upper intermediate group.

> *a cockroach   a brand new pair of jeans   a bowl of soup*
>
> *the first time I'd taught them   I felt really embarrassed*
>
> *a massive hole   it got bigger and bigger!*
>
> *it was so horrible!   I suddenly realized   my friend's house*

2 Ask the learners in pairs to discuss what the two possible stories could be.
3 Invite one or two pairs to share their ideas with the rest of the class.
4 Now ask the class to vote on which of the two stories they would prefer to hear (in my case a story about a cockroach or one about a brand new pair of jeans).
5 Tell them their chosen story in as natural a way as possible, recording yourself as you do it.
6 Allow any responses to the story to surface, and then ask the learners to retell it orally in pairs.
7 Play the recording of the story and ask the class to make a note of any useful areas of language that they heard. Make a note of language areas yourself while they do this.
8 Ask everyone to share what they wrote down in small groups, and then write up some of the most important things they found on the board.
9 Bring everyone together and check comprehension of what is on the board. You may also wish to introduce some language areas that you wrote down yourself at this stage.

4.4 Letters to the class

Memory focus	Encouraging learners to recall and reprocess information and language which have been introduced through student–teacher interaction.
Level	Beginners–pre-intermediate
Time	30 minutes plus
Preparation	Write a letter to the class containing information about yourself that is focused around a particular topic and/or area of language (Letter A). Now make another version of the letter where about 10 items of information have been changed (Letter B). Each learner needs a copy of both letters. The example in Box 4.4 is for a beginner-level class.

Procedure

1   Invite the class to ask you questions about your life, directing them towards the particular areas that the letter is about. With a low-level group, these questions may happen at least partly in the mother tongue. In this case, reformulate each question into English before providing your answer, making sure that everything is at a level that is accessible for the learners, and using mime and translation where necessary to illustrate meanings. Make sure all the areas of the letter get covered.

2   Give out copies of Letter B (the incorrect version). Ask everyone to underline and change everything that they think is incorrect. They then compare ideas in pairs.

3   Now give out copies of Letter A (the correct version) so that they can check their work.

4   Using Letter A as a model, learners write a letter about themselves that is focused on the same area.

Box 4.4: Letters to the class

Letter A

Dear Class,

My name is Carmen Paredes. Now I live in Santiago, but I'm originally from the South of Chile. I'm 45 years old. I'm your English teacher. Welcome to this class!

I live in a small flat in Providencia with my husband and my children. I have one son and one daughter. My husband works in a shop. My son is a student at university. He's studying art. My daughter goes to primary school. She's nine years old.

I come to school by bike every day. It takes about 20 minutes.

I can speak Spanish, English and a little German.

I like going to the cinema and playing tennis and football.

I hope you enjoy this class!

Carmen

Letter B

Dear Class,

My name is Carmen Paredes. Now I live in Santiago, but I'm originally from the North of Chile. I'm 55 years old. I'm your English teacher. Welcome to this class!

I live in a big house in Providencia with my husband and my children. I have one son and one daughter. My wife works in a restaurant. My son is a student at university. He's studying mathematics. My daughter goes to secondary school. She's nine years old.

I come to school by bus every day. It takes about 50 minutes.

I can speak Spanish, English and a little French.

I like going to the cinema and playing basketball and football.

I hope you enjoy this class!

Carmen

4.5 Choral chanting

Memory focus	Saying a poem or chant repeatedly so that it can be produced fluently.
Level	Any
Time	5–10 minutes in each class
Preparation	Choose a poem or chant with a strong pattern of rhythm and rhyme (see an example in Box 4.5). Prepare to project it or write it on the board.

Procedure

1 Write the text on the board, or display it on a projector.
2 Read it out loudly and clearly, focusing on natural rhythm and varying the way you use your voice to make it interesting to listen to.
3 Read each line again with the class repeating after you.
4 Assign different parts of the text to different groups of learners. With the text in Box 4.5, for instance, a large group of learners can read the narrator's part, another group can read the part of Tiddler, and individuals can read the parts of the teacher and the other fish.
5 In the next class, perform the text with the class again, perhaps varying which learners read which parts. If learners enjoy this text and have developed a reasonable level of fluency in their delivery, you could move on to a different part of the story.

Box 4.5: Choral chanting

Once there was a fish and his name was Tiddler.
He wasn't much to look at, with his plain grey scales.
But Tiddler was a fish with a big imagination.
He blew small bubbles but he told tall tales.

"Sorry I'm late. I was riding on a seahorse."
"Sorry I'm late. I was flying with a ray."
"Sorry I'm late. I was diving with a dolphin."
Tiddler told a different story every day.

At nine o'clock on Monday, Miss Skate called the register.
"Little Johnny Dory?" "Yes, Miss Skate."
"Rabbitfish?" "Yes, Miss." "Redfin?" "Yes, Miss."
"Tiddler? Tiddler?" "TIDDLER'S LATE!"

"Sorry I'm late. I was swimming round a shipwreck.
I swam into a treasure chest, and someone closed the lid.
I bashed and I thrashed till a mermaid let me out again."
"Oh no she didn't!" "OH YES SHE DID!"

"It's only a story," said Rabbitfish and Redfin.
"Just a silly story," said Dragonfish and Dab.
"I *like* Tiddler's story," said Little Johnny Dory,
And he told it to his granny, who told it to a crab.

© Scholastic 2007

From *Memory Activities for Language Learning*
© Cambridge University Press 2011   PHOTOCOPIABLE

4.6 The next word

Memory focus	Encouraging learners to notice, store and retrieve the language of texts in chunks.
Level	Any
Time	10 minutes plus
Preparation	Find a short text that the learners have already worked with (from a previous unit of the coursebook, for example).

Procedure

1   Read through the text slowly, stopping at various points and asking the learners to shout out what they think the next word is. A good place to make these breaks is in the middle of a chunk of language. For instance, in the text from *English in Mind Student's Book 1*, Second edition by Herbert Puchta and Jeff Stranks in Box 4.6, some suitable places to stop could be after the words *sometimes*, *little*, *difficult*, or any of the other words in the first sentence. When someone guesses the next word correctly, repeat the chunk and then continue on to the next gap. It would work something like this:

Teacher:	It can sometimes …
Student 1:	feel
Teacher:	(shakes head)
Student 2:	be
Teacher:	It can sometimes be a little …
Student 3:	difficult
Teacher:	It can sometimes be a little difficult to learn a …

2 When you have worked through the whole text in this way, ask the learners to work in pairs. They now do the same activity: one learner looks at the original text in the coursebook and reads part of it, and the other learner tries to guess the next word.

Tip: You can make this process easier by reading the text through once to the learners immediately before doing the activity.

Variation
Change some of the words of the text as you read it out so that instead of supplying the next word, learners have to correct what you have said.

Box 4.6: The next word

It can sometimes be a little difficult to learn a foreign language fluently. But there are many things you can do to make your learning more successful. When you speak a foreign language, it's normal to have an accent. That's OK – other people can usually understand. It's a good idea to listen to CDs and try to imitate other speakers to make your pronunciation better.

If you see a new word, and you don't know what it means, you can sometimes guess the meaning from words you know, or you can look up the word in a dictionary.

A lot of good language learners try not to translate things from their first language. Translation is sometimes a good idea, but try to think in the foreign language if you can!

It's also normal to make mistakes. When your teacher corrects a mistake in your writing or speaking, think about it and try to see why it's wrong. But it's more important to communicate, so don't be afraid to speak!

© Cambridge University Press 2010

From *Memory Activities for Language Learning*
© Cambridge University Press 2011   PHOTOCOPIABLE

Some ways to revisit a short text

1   Dictate the text to the learners but ask them to write down only the first and last letters of each word. They then work in pairs and try to reconstruct it orally, just by looking at what they have written. They can then check by looking at the book if necessary. Which pair managed to do it by checking the least number of times?

2   Read part of the text to the class at faster than dictation speed. When you have finished, the learners make a note of any words or chunks that they remember. They then use these in pairs to try to reconstruct a text which is as close to the original as possible.

3   Put up multiple copies of the text on the classroom walls. Learners walk to the wall, remember a short part of the text exactly, and then walk back and write it down on a piece of paper. This process continues until all of the text has been copied to their notebooks.

4   As above, but instead of writing the text themselves when they get back from the wall, learners dictate it to a partner who remains sitting. The learners can swap roles halfway through the activity. When they finish, they check their work for accuracy before comparing it with the original text.

5   Write out the complete text on the board. Ask one learner to read it out. Now ask another learner to tell you three random words from the text. Rub these three words out and ask the learner to read the complete text but to include the words that have disappeared. Keep repeating this process with different learners until the class are staring at a blank board and have retained the complete text in their heads.

6   Give out the text and ask the learners to write a comprehension question for it which they think their teacher will not be able to answer. They then share these in groups and decide on the most difficult one to ask in front of the whole class. The class can beat the teacher if he or she answers more questions incorrectly than correctly. The teacher is not allowed to review the text beforehand.

7   After doing a few examples as a class, learners go through the text and underline everything that they would say is a language chunk. Then in small groups, they share what they have underlined and check the accuracy of their work in dictionaries or online corpora. Other things to underline could be words that they particularly like or dislike, words that are high priority for them to remember, words of three syllables, words of a particular word class (e.g. adjectives), words that they do not think it is important to remember.

8   Ask learners in small groups to try to sing as much of the text as they can to the tune of their national anthem, or a popular song that they know. Those groups who want to can then perform it to the rest of the class.

4.7 I can't spell that!

Memory focus	Making spellings memorable through noticing and retrieval activities.
Level	Any
Time	15 minutes plus (depending on the length of the text)
Preparation	Choose a short text or dialogue to be reviewed. This could be one that has already been encountered by the learners, but which is above their active level of language.

Procedure

1 Direct the learners to the relevant page of the coursebook, or give out copies of the text. Ask them to reread the text, telling them that later you will be dictating it to them. Ask them to go through it and underline any words which they think they may spell incorrectly during the dictation stage. They now discuss these with a partner, predicting how many mistakes they think they will make.

2 The learners spend a few minutes practising the areas that they think they will have difficulties with. This may involve looking at a word, looking away and trying to rewrite it, and then looking back at the text to check.

3 They turn over the text and any papers they have used to practise on, and the teacher dictates the text whilst the learners write it out. For a greater challenge, the text can be dictated at a later point in the lesson, or even on a different day.

4 The learners look back at the original text and compare their predictions with the number of mistakes actually made. They then discuss this again in pairs.

Note

For many learners the process of thinking about mistakes that will be made is a step towards greater accuracy. The predicted number of mistakes is usually higher than the number actually made.

4.8 Spontaneous translation

Memory focus	Retrieving a short text in the target language, through the medium of the mother tongue (L1).
Level	Elementary and above
Time	10 minutes plus
Preparation	Rewrite the short text (or part of it) or dialogue to be reviewed so that it is in the L1 of the class. Make copies of both texts so that there is enough for everyone in the class. This activity is most suitable for monolingual groups. For working with a multilingual group, see Activity 4.9: *Retranslated text*, which works along similar lines.

Procedure

1 Learners work in pairs. Initially just give a copy of the L1 translation of the text to Learner A in each pair, and the English text to Learner B. They should not show their texts to each other.

2 Learner A looks at the L1 version and orally translates it bit by bit into English. Learner B listens and provides feedback on the accuracy of what Learner A is saying, giving occasional words as prompts if Learner A gets stuck.

3 The texts and roles can now be swapped around. It should of course be much easier for Learner B to perform this task having very recently seen the English version. For this reason, it is better if the stronger of the two learners goes first.

4 Now give out the extra texts so that everyone has both copies. Learners now go through the English version together and reflect on which bits were the most difficult and on how well they performed the task. Invite them to share some of these issues with the whole class.

Variation
For some lower-level learners, it may be more appropriate to begin by doing the exercise the other way around (i.e. translate from English to L1 first). This is generally much easier.

Note
Of course there will be ways of translating the L1 text into English which are different from the written English version. This is perfectly acceptable, and it will be useful for learners to compare and contrast these with what is written. You will need to be available to deal with any queries about accuracy.

4.9 Retranslated text

Memory focus	Reconstructing a text in the target language by using the mother tongue (L1) as a memory trigger.
Level	Elementary and above
Time	2 × 10 minutes plus (depending on the length of the text)
Preparation	Access to a short text that learners have already encountered. As with the preceding activity, this works best with texts that are up to only five sentences in length.

Procedure

1 Give each learner a copy of the text, or show them where it is in the coursebook.
2 Ask them to rewrite the text in their L1. Emphasize that they should translate the ideas of the text into the most natural L1 version that they can, rather than word for word. When everyone has finished, ask them to write their names on the papers and collect them in.
3 In the next class, or after a suitable amount of time has passed, give each learner back their own L1 version of the text. Making sure that the English version of the text is not in sight, now ask everyone to rewrite their L1 version into English. Here's an example done by Régis, a pre-intermediate learner in Brazil, using the first paragraph of the short text from *English in Mind* used in Box 4.6.

> Sometimes can be a little difficult to learn a foreign language fluently. But there are many things you can do to make your learning more succefuly. When you speak a foreign language, it is normal have an accent. That's OK – other people can usually understand. It's a good idea listen CDs and try copy others speakers to make your pronunciation better.

4 Now ask the learners to compare their version of the text in English with the original English version. Which parts did they translate accurately? Where there are differences, was an acceptable alternative used? Learners discuss these questions in small groups.
5 Ask everyone to make a note of a few areas of language that they failed to produce accurately in this exercise. Can they come up with their own personalized examples to practise these areas? For example, for the text above, Régis could focus on the chunks *it's normal to (do something), it's a good idea to (do something), it can be a little difficult to (do something),* which were all produced incorrectly in his initial retranslation.

4.10 Creating still images

Memory focus	Encouraging learners to remember events, relationships and emotions in stories they have read or heard.
Level	Pre-intermediate and above
Time	20 minutes plus
Preparation	The learners need to have all read or listened to the same story or the same part of a story.

Procedure

1 Ask the learners to work in small groups and talk about specific moments from the story that they remember. You may want to help them with this by giving an example yourself.

2 Choose your own moment in the story and tell the class about it. Ask for a volunteer for each of the characters involved in the scene. Discuss with the class where the characters are, what positions they are in, the expressions on their faces, etc. Now mould the volunteers into the desired 'image' by telling them what posture and attitude to assume until everyone is happy with the still image you have created.

3 Ask them to plan some still images in their groups to show some or all of the moments they had discussed (see the example in Box 4.10). Allow them time to try them out.

4 Ask learners to show their still images. Invite comment from other groups on which scene they feel is being portrayed and how it compares to their own interpretation of the scene.

Follow-up

1 Choose one of the scenes to work with in more detail and invite the participants to present it again at the front of the class. Ask some of the characters to leave the scene so that only one is remaining. This character maintains his or her position. Different learners now come up to the front and stand behind the character. As they do so, they say what they feel the character is thinking at this moment. When there are several people behind the main character, the character decides which of the sentences he or she most identifies with. Move these voices closer to the character. Now 'conduct' the voices by pointing at them and asking them to speak. As with an orchestra, the voices may be used on numerous occasions. Use voices that are closest to the character more frequently than those that are further away.

Learners can now go back to their groups and prepare similar 'sound sculptures' for other moments in the story. These are then presented to the rest of the class. This idea comes from the work of the German Drama in Education specialist, Ingo Scheller. See the References and further reading section at the end of the book for details of his published work.

2   Ask learners to script or improvise a short scene using one of their still images as a starting point. These can then be presented to the rest of the class.

Box 4.10: Creating still images

From *Memory Activities for Language Learning*
© Cambridge University Press 2011   PHOTOCOPIABLE

4.11 Who said it? When?

Memory focus	Encouraging learners to revisit the dialogue in a graded reader and the context around it.
Level	Pre-intermediate and above
Time	15 minutes plus
Preparation	Make sure everyone has a graded reader to hand that they have read and enjoyed. It should be a story with at least three different characters.

Procedure

1   In pairs, learners swap their graded readers.
2   Each person now copies out some interesting lines of dialogue from the text that they have been given, and next to each line writes the name of the character who said it.
3   When they have done this, ask pairs to test each other by saying the line to them. Their partners should then say which character said the line and, if possible, at which point in the story it was said.

Note
I learnt this technique from Frøydis Solberg, a teacher of English and Norwegian for immigrants in Norway.

Variation
At higher levels, this activity can also be done with films. Each pair of learners agrees on a film that they have both enjoyed and then try to find the film script on the internet. They then each write a list of lines of dialogue as in the main activity. Neither person needs to have seen the film in English. (They may have seen only a dubbed version.) A good source of film scripts is available at http://www.script-o-rama.com/, but they can also be found by typing the name of the film and the words 'film script' into an internet search engine.

4.12 That's not how I wrote it

Memory focus	Raising awareness about differences between a learner's text and a reworked version of the same text.
Level	Elementary and above
Time	15 minutes plus
Preparation	Give the learners a short writing task (up to 150 words) to do in class. See Box 4.12 for an example used with a pre-intermediate group. When learners have finished, collect them in, or ask learners to email them to you. Now write out a new version of each text at home, making it more accurate and/or using more complex language. (This will be easier to do if you have received their texts in digital form.) The reworking of the text should be done at a level which is not too far above that of each individual student. See the examples in Box 4.12.

Procedure

1 As soon as possible after the students have done the writing task (preferably in the next lesson when it is still fresh in their minds), give each learner the reformulated versions of their own texts. Ask them to underline areas where they think their original text was different in terms of vocabulary, grammar, spelling, punctuation, paragraphing, etc.
2 Ask the learners to discuss what they have underlined. How is it different and why do they think the change was made?
3 Now give out their original pieces of writing to compare with the reformulated versions and ask them to underline any outstanding differences.
4 The learners work in the same pairs again to discuss why they think each change has been made. Be available to deal with any outstanding queries.

Variation
Take in all of the learners' original texts after the writing stage and read out a spontaneously reworked version of each one to the class. Then give them back their own pieces of writing and ask them to underline areas where they felt that your spoken version differed. This version is only feasible with small classes.

Follow-up
If a data projector is available, and the texts exist in electronic format, both versions of one text can be projected side by side for the whole class to see.

Differences can then be discussed and compared. The texts can then be removed and the learners asked to reconstruct the improved version from memory.

In a future class, ask the learners to focus on the original versions of their texts and to attempt to improve them in the light of what they can remember from the reworked versions (making sure these versions are out of the way first).

Box 4.12: That's not how I wrote it

Write a letter to a friend describing the place where you are studying English, and asking about his or her new job. Write 70–90 words.

Original piece of writing

Dear Marcia,

I hope your right. my college is a old build, there is lot's of classes and that is central languages. If you want to improve your English or you intrested in other languages I suggest to come this college and use class because that would be good for you. Now can I ask some question form your new job? where did you get this job? How many hours you work? Do you like this job and what kind of job is it?

Parisa

Reformulated version

Dear Marcia,

I hope you're alright. My college is an old building with lots of classes and it's a language centre. If you want to improve your English, or you're interested in other languages, I suggest that you come to this college because it would be good for you.

Now can I ask some questions about your new job? Where did you get this job? How many hours a week do you work? Do you like it and what kind of job is it?

Parisa

4.13 Holiday snaps

Memory focus	Learners speak spontaneously and creatively about holiday pictures and then improve on their speech through task repetition.
Level	Pre-intermediate and above
Time	15 minutes plus
Preparation	Find about 16 pictures that look as though they could be someone's holiday snaps showing a wide range of different places, people and activities, e.g. from http://www.flickr.com/ or http://images.google.co.uk/imghp?hl=en&tab+wi Paste these onto two separate PowerPoint® presentations so that there are around 8 on each. Set up the presentations so that there is a time lag of 20 seconds between each image. (See Boxes 4.13a and 4.13b for photos from the two example presentations on the CD-ROM for Variation 2 below.)

Procedure

1   Ask the learners to work in pairs. The first PowerPoint presentation is displayed on the projector and put into slide-show mode. Everyone needs to be able to see the pictures clearly. Learner A talks about each picture as it comes up, as if it were their own holiday snap. For example:

> Well, this is one of my boyfriend. We were on holiday in Australia and we were on our way to visit my sister, but the car broke down and we had to fix it. We couldn't go any further, so we had to camp by the side of the road, but it was a really beautiful place and . . .

2   Learner B now does the same thing with the second presentation.
3   Each Learner A now swaps places with another Learner A from a different pair. The presentations are shown again, and both Learners A and B repeat their talks. This process can be repeated several times.

Variations

1   The learners prepare presentations for each other to talk about.
2   The presentations are set up so that the time lag between images is longer in the first or the second showing. If the first showing has 20-second gaps (see Box 4.13a on the CD-ROM) and the second has 10 (see Box 4.13b on the CD-ROM), the learners are challenged to speak more fluently, using more complex forms, the second time around. If, on the other hand, the second showing is longer than the first, then this will require the learners to expand on the details of their stories.

Box 4.13a: Holiday snaps

From *Memory Activities for Language Learning*
© Cambridge University Press 2011   PHOTOCOPIABLE

Box 4.13b: Holiday snaps

From *Memory Activities for Language Learning*
© Cambridge University Press 2011   PHOTOCOPIABLE

3   The learners see the images and have a chance to plan (perhaps as homework) before they need to talk about them.
4   With a small class, just one longer presentation can be shown and the learners take it in turns to talk about each image.

Note
The idea of talking through PowerPoint slides to a preset timer comes from the presentation technique of *PechaKucha* (see http://www.pecha-kucha.org/). *PowerPoint karaoke* (see: http://blog.slideshare.net/2007/07/11/slideshare-karoake-randomizer) is the term used when the speaker is unaware of what the content of the slides will be.

    To create your own presentation, you will need suitable software installed on your computer. PowerPoint (see http://www.microsoft.com/ for pricing options) is the most popular program and Impress (see http://www.openoffice.org/) is a free alternative.

If you simply want to use the example presentations on the CD-ROM, Microsoft offers the free PowerPoint Viewer, and OpenOffice also has a free viewing program.

4.14 Exaggerated accidents

Memory focus	Holding the details of a story in working memory and noticing differences between tellings of the same story.
Level	Intermediate and above
Time:	30 minutes plus
Preparation	None

Procedure

1 Ask the learners to recall a time when they had a small accident. It could be falling off a bike as a child on their way to school or something more recent. Tell them that they are going to tell the story of their accident to one other person. Emphasize to them that it does not have to be a very interesting story. Ask them to spend a minute or two planning, by remembering the details of what happened and possibly making a few notes.

2 The learners work in groups of four or five. Within each group they should decide who is A, B, C and D. If there are five people in a group, then two learners work as one of the letters together, and take turns in the storytelling stages.

3 A and B work together. C and D work together. They tell their stories to each other. The person who is listening tries to remember the details of the other person's story. If there are two people working as the same letter, then only one of them tells a story. Allow everyone time to finish.

4 A and C work together. B and D work together. They now tell each other the story they just heard – not their own story! However, they should tell it as if it actually happened to them (i.e. in the first person). They should also exaggerate it slightly.

5 A and D work together. B and C work together. Again they tell each other the story they just heard, as if it had happened to them and, again, exaggerating it. The stories have now returned to their original tellers – albeit somewhat changed!

6 Initiate a feedback session. How did the learners feel when their original stories came back to them? In what ways had the stories changed?

Note

It can be a very nice boost to the learners' confidence to have a story which started out as something quite simple come back to them with all the makings of a Hollywood blockbuster!

4.15 Repeated role plays

Memory focus	Improving performance in role play through task repetition.
Level	Pre-intermediate and above
Time	10 minutes plus
Preparation	None

Procedure

1 Ask everyone to stand up and find a partner. If there is an odd number of learners, there should be one group of three. Ask each pair to decide which one of them will play the role of travel agent and which one the role of a customer booking a holiday. They should remember both the person they are working with and the roles they have agreed on.

2 Now everyone finds a different partner. This time one of them is a mechanic and one of them has a problem with his or her car. Again they should remember what they have decided.

3 Now everyone finds a different partner again. This time one of them works in an electrical shop and the other is a customer.

4 Now tell the learners that you are going to call out a number – 1, 2 or 3 – referring to each of the three role plays. They should then try to find their partner for that number as quickly as possible and start the role play. When you call out a different number, they should move to the appropriate person and start that role play instead. Keep moving them around fairly briskly, but let them experience each role-play situation two or three times. Emphasize that each time they go back to the same person, they should restart the conversation from the beginning.

5 After a few minutes stop the role-play activity. Call out the numbers one more time so that they can find each partner and reflect on the experience. In what ways was each version of the role play different? Did they feel that there were any improvements made in terms of their use of language?

Follow-up

Elicit from the class some useful terms and expressions that came out of each role-play scenario and write them on the board.

Note

This idea is based on the work of David Heathfield. For more examples
of quick-change role-play activities, see his book *Spontaneous Speaking:
Drama Activities for Confidence and Fluency*, Peaslake: Delta Publishing,
2005.

4.16 Whose story is it?

Memory focus	Task repetition of personal stories.
Level	Pre-intermediate and above
Time	30 minutes plus
Preparation	Choose some topics for the class to tell personal stories about. Depending on the group, these could include *my first day at school, getting lost, a nightmare journey, an embarrassing moment, an experience of culture shock, a moment of pride, a time of confusion*, etc.

Procedure

1 Write the topics for the talks on the board. Ask everyone to choose one of
the topics that they would feel comfortable talking about and to prepare
to talk about it for a few minutes, making notes if they want to.

2 Put the learners into groups of two or three. Everyone tells their stories to
each other.

3 Now tell everyone that they can choose either to retell their own story or
to tell one of the stories that they have heard as if it had happened to them.
Allow them a few minutes to check the details of each other's story.

4 Now put each group together with another one to make larger groups of
four to six. Learners either tell their own story again in the new group or
tell one of the stories that they have heard as if it had happened to them.
At the end of each telling, those who are listening to the stories for the
first time guess which person is the original storyteller.

Variation

Learners initially prepare to tell their stories in three minutes. When they are
ready, they work with a partner and swap stories. Now ask them to retell
their stories, but this time in two minutes. Finally, ask them to do it again in
just a minute. Decreasing the time limit each time encourages a more fluent
telling of the stories.

4.17 The listeners

Memory focus	Encouraging more reflection in speaking activities by asking learners to remember and give feedback on each other's utterances.
Level	Pre-intermediate and above
Time	20 minutes plus
Preparation	Make a set of the statements in Box 4.17a for each group of three or four learners.

Procedure

1   Organize the class into groups of three or four.
2   Give each group a set of the statements. Ask them to place them face down on the table.
3   Learners take it in turns to take one of the statements and read it out. They then discuss in their group what they think about the topic. One person should keep out of the conversation, but listen very carefully to everything that is said. When they have run out of things to say, the listener gives feedback to the group about what was said and by whom.
4   This is repeated with each of the topics, but with a different person taking the role of listener each time. Of course it is natural that some of the topics will promote more discussion than others.
5   At the end, everyone writes down a list of some of the things that were said by different people during the discussion.
6   Everyone reads out their lists and the others try to recall who said each utterance.

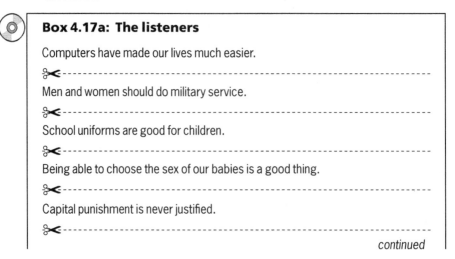

Box 4.17a: The listeners

Computers have made our lives much easier.

✂ --

Men and women should do military service.

✂ --

School uniforms are good for children.

✂ --

Being able to choose the sex of our babies is a good thing.

✂ --

Capital punishment is never justified.

✂ --

continued

Box 4.17a: (*cont.*)

Money is the root of all evil.

✂ --

Hunting and bullfighting are cruel and should be banned.

✂ --

It's better to buy things in small shops than in supermarkets.

✂ --

Tourism has more advantages than disadvantages.

✂ --

We should protect languages that are dying out.

✂ --

Sportsmen and women get paid too much money.

✂ --

If you work hard in life you will be successful.

✂ --

Advertising aimed at children should be illegal.

✂ --

Hospitals and universities should be free for everyone.

✂ --

Smoking should be banned in all public places.

✂ --

The government should be able to control what gets printed in newspapers.

✂ --

Violence on television causes violence in society.

✂ --

It's better to have children before you reach thirty.

✂ --

The more security cameras there are the better.

✂ --

The media shouldn't print details of celebrities' private lives.

Variation

Summaries of discussions like this can also be written on the class blog so that they can be accessed and commented on by everyone in the class later. See Box 4.17b for an example provided by Chia Suan Chong.

Box 4.17b: The listeners

Then after the break, while doing corrections, we started to talk about how intonation can cause misunderstanding, which led to a discussion on how intonation, volume and pitch can carry different meanings or connotations in different countries. Maha informed us that in Arabic, the range of intonation change is quite narrow, while in Japan, a wider range of intonation suggests informality and being over-emotive. This spurred a discussion about whether expressing one's emotions was acceptable in your different countries. While the people of the UK, Korea and Japan took pride in hiding emotions, seeing this as strength of character, the Spanish and Brazilians clearly appreciated the honesty of emotions and saw it as a sign of a trustworthy person ... What a difference culture can make!

We also discussed how tactile people were in our countries and how men and women greeted each other, which led one group to start talking about gender differences – a very interesting topic I hope we can explore tomorrow ...

Anyway, feel free to continue the very interesting discussions we had in class today here.

Looking forward to reading your comments!

Chia

---

5   Memory techniques and mnemonics

Elena Ferragud, a teacher of English to teenagers in Spain, noticed one day that despite having taught and corrected the point many times, lots of people in the class could not seem to remember the standard pronunciation of the word *comfortable*. Then she suddenly had an idea. She wrote on the board two English words that everyone knew very well already – *come* and *football*. Through linking the sounds of these words with *comfortable*, the class were immediately able to achieve much more accurate pronunciation. Not only that, they were also able to remember the pronunciation when the word came up again in later classes.

What Elena was doing was making use of a mnemonic – an age-old way of making what is difficult to remember easier by linking it to something that is already well stored, or easy to store in long-term memory. Often, as in the example above, there is no natural connection between the content of the mnemonic (*come* and *football*) with the item to be learnt (*comfortable*), but it is the creation of this connection that serves as a memory trigger.

Mnemonics can be verbally focused, visually focused, or both. They can be single-use strategies for remembering particular meanings, spellings or pronunciation, or they can be more generative in nature, to be used as a tool whenever new things need to be learnt. All of these mnemonic types are relevant and useful to the teaching and learning of foreign languages.

Verbal mnemonics work with the principle that language items can be stored according to associations they have with words with similar spellings or sounds. For example, to remember the 13 French verbs that take the verb *être*, we might remember the acronym V. A. T. NERD. Each letter of the acronym stands for one of the verbs and its opposite (*retourner* has no opposite).

venir – aller
arriver – partir
tomber – rester
naître – mourir
entrer – sortir
retourner
descendre – monter

Mnemonics like this are good for reminding us of linguistic form (in this case the first letter of the verbs) but do not tell us anything about the meanings of the words. For remembering meanings, visual mnemonics usually work better. For instance, for the above list of verbs we could draw a picture of a house with different stick people doing each of the 13 actions, or ask learners to imagine the actions happening in different parts of their own houses. Visual mnemonics make use of the fact that images tend to be fairly easy to recall, but they may give no clues as to pronunciation or spelling.

The 'keyword memory technique' has become one of the most widely used memory techniques for foreign-language study and incorporates both visual and verbal mnemonics. Supposing you would like to remember the French word for *fall* (*tomber*). We need first to find a mother-tongue word which is somehow similar in form, to use as a link. Let's use the English word *tomb*. Now we need to create a memorable image which will connect the meaning of the French word with the meaning of the English link word. One way of doing this could be to imagine a ghostly picture of a man falling slowly into a tomb.

The activities in this chapter demonstrate a number of ways of using verbal and visual mnemonics as well as other memory techniques for remembering language. They are activities which can be used in class with the goal of helping learners to learn specific items, but they can also raise awareness about the value of mnemonics and serve as models for strategies for independent self-study.

5.1 Chants

Memory focus	Making connected, rhythmic speech memorable through chanting. (See also Activity 2.10: *Celebrity rhyming poems*.)
Level	Any
Time	5 minutes plus
Preparation	None

Procedure

1   Chant a text like the one below to the class. You can help the learners to notice the rhythm by clicking your fingers or tapping on the desk. Ask everyone to repeat each line after you. This could be done purely through the sounds, but if you think seeing the written form will help with comprehension, then write it on the board too.

One, two, three,
I'd like a cup of tea.
Four, five, six,
I'd like a plate of chips.
Seven, eight, nine,
I'd like a glass of wine.

2   Now do it again, but this time you say the numbers and ask the class to respond by supplying the other parts.
3   Now ask half the class to say the numbers while the rest respond. Swap these roles around.

Note
The chant above is suitable for a low-level group, but the same counting chant can also be used to encourage natural connected speech for a wide range of other structures. For instance, for a higher-level group you could try the following:

One, two, three,
Is anyone making a cup of tea?
Four, five, six,
I could murder a plate of chips.
Seven, eight, nine,
What I'd like is a glass of wine.

Here are some other examples of areas of language that can be used with this chant.

Can I have …?	Would you like …?	I'm going to have …,
Have you had …?	Shall we have …?	I've been having a …,
Let's have …,	Did you have …?	Can someone bring me …?
What I'd like is …,	I'd like to order …?	Would anyone like …?

Putting language into a chant format is a good way to make language stick. When designing chants for use in the classroom, the following guidelines may be useful:

- Use short lines with a strong rhythm.
- Include formulaic language (chunks), functional language and/or repeated grammatical structure.
- Build in rhyme (if possible).
- Make them dialogic (if possible – i.e. so that one half of the class can chant to the other half).

The names of letters

Knowing the names of the letters in the languages we are learning is very useful for spelling out loud our names and addresses and other words. However, we can often be over-influenced by the names of the letters in our mother tongue, so anything that we can do to help to make the names stick in English can be very useful. The 'Alphabet' song below, sung to the tune of 'Twinkle, Twinkle Little Star', can be presented and learnt by heart as a way of making the sound of all of the letter names memorable.

- A, B, C, D, E, F, G (Twinkle, twinkle little star)
- H, I, J, K, L, M, N, O, P (How I wonder what you are)
- Q, R, S, T, U, V (Up above the world so high)
- W, X, Y, Z (Like a diamond in the sky)
- Now you know your ABC (Twinkle Twinkle little star)
- Next time won't you sing with me? (How I wonder what you are)

It is also helpful to group letters with the same vowel sound together and to present them in this way, or to ask learners to sort them into the different categories.

- A, H, J, K   eɪ
- B, C, D, E, G, P, T, V   iː
- F, L, M, N, S, X, Z   e
- I, Y   aɪ
- O   əʊ
- Q, U, W   juː
- R   aː

For individual letters, linking the sound of the letter to words that contain both the sound and the letter works well. For example:

- A   say, day
- B   be
- E   email, easy
- I   I am a student, iPod
- K, O, R and U   R U OK? (Are you OK?)

5.2 Put it in my pocket

Memory focus	Making language items memorable by linking them to unusual places.
Level	Any
Time	5 minutes
Preparation	None

Procedure

1 When you have a set of words or chunks to review, write them up all over the board in a random fashion.
2 Now rub out one of the language items on the board and, as you do so, mime taking it and placing it somewhere in your clothing or on your body. For instance, you could take the first one and pretend to place it in your back pocket, and then take the next one and put it in your ear, etc. Provide commentary for what you are doing as you do it, e.g. *I'm taking 'fed up' and I'm putting it in my shoe.*
3 When you have done up to 10 of these, call out all the language items again and ask the class to recall where each one is. Alternatively, for an extra challenge, go through the locations again and ask the learners to recall the language item that was placed there.

Variation
You can also incorporate the physical world of the students into this activity. For instance, *I'm putting 'punctual' under Ingrid's bag*, and so on.

Note
I learnt the idea of putting words from the board into different items of clothing from Chris Roland at the British Council, Barcelona. This idea, like 'Technique 2' in Activity 5.8: *Memory technique swap* (see Box 5.8b on p. 156), is a variation of the 'loci memory technique' which dates back to Ancient Greece.

5.3 Where's the link?

Memory focus	Encouraging learners to create memorable links between language items.
Level	Elementary and above
Time	5–10 minutes
Preparation	None

Procedure

1   At some point in a lesson, you may have a number of seemingly unrelated language items written up on the board like this.

> *a lump   a lobster   get into a panic   regret (something)*
> *a bit of a mess   Christmas decorations   get flooded out*
> *over-optimistic   in his fifties   in a good mood*

Bring everyone together so that they are focusing on the board.

2   Choose two of the language items and establish a way of linking the items together (see examples in Step 3).

3   After doing a few examples together, ask the class to work in pairs to put the items into a logical order and to discuss a possible link between each item. For example:

> The girl got a lump on her head when the lobster fell on it.
> The lobster got into a panic when it was caught by the fisherman.
> If you get into a panic, you regret it afterwards.
> The house is a bit of a mess, so you're regretting having the children's party.
> The children pulled down the Christmas decorations, so it's a bit of a mess.
> The Christmas decorations got wet when you got flooded out.
> The man was over-optimistic about the rain stopping. Eventually he got flooded out.
> The woman was over-optimistic about finding a younger husband. Actually she married someone in his fifties.
> The best time of his life was when he was in his fifties. He was always in a good mood.

3   When they have finished, ask them to go back through the words in the same order, remembering the link they discussed before.

4   Now ask them to try to recall all of the items in order without looking at the board.

Variation

Learners work in pairs. One person picks two of the language items and the other person has to think quickly of a way of linking the two items. For instance:

A: lobster ... in his fifties

B: When my uncle was in his fifties he started eating lobster every day. a lump ... in a good mood

A: I'm in a really good mood because there aren't any lumps in my milkshake.

5.4 The story method

Memory focus	Making language memorable by creating a story around it.
Level	Pre-intermediate and above
Time	10 minutes plus
Preparation	Write out a list of language items to be reviewed, or new language to be focused on, and make a copy for each group of learners. See Box 5.4 for a list of expressions using *look* suitable for a pre-intermediate and above group.

Procedure

1 Organize the class into pairs or small groups. Give each group a set of the language items cut into strips.

2 Each group goes through the items together, checking that they understand the meanings and agreeing on a logical order. They should try to create a story using as many of the language items as possible. You may wish to establish the tense that the story will be told in.

3 Everyone now makes sure that they can remember the story well enough to retell it, either by mentally going over it again, or by retelling it among themselves.

4 Reorganize the class so that people from different groups are working together. Ask them to share their stories with each other.

Box 5.4: The story method

Look up to (somebody)

✂---

Look after (somebody or something)

✂---

Look forward to (something)

✂---

Look (something) up

✂---

Look into (something)

✂---

Look around (somewhere)

✂---

Look like (something or somebody)

✂---

Look down on (somebody)

✂---

Look for (something or somebody)

✂---

Look at (something or somebody)

✂---

Look out!

✂---

I'm just looking.

✂---

Look after yourself

✂---

Look where you're going!

From *Memory Activities for Language Learning*
© Cambridge University Press 2011   PHOTOCOPIABLE

Variations

1   Ask each pair to write their story out. The stories can be passed around or stuck up around the room and commented on by other learners.
2   Using a list of words which begin with the same letter (e.g. *policeman, peach, panic, polite*, etc.) or rhyming words (*hair, chair, unfair, over there*, etc.) in a story can produce amusing results. Words containing a particular sound that the learners find challenging can be chosen, for example, lists of rhyming words (see Activity 2.10: *Celebrity rhyming poems*).

Angelica's story

Angelica Fernando took a diploma in Japanese at the School of Oriental and African Studies in London, progressing from complete beginner to advanced level in a period of a year. Being fascinated by Japanese culture and having a real thirst for listening to Japanese songs, watching films and understanding newspapers really helped her to keep her motivation for learning new things about the language, but she also found that she needed some memory techniques to remember new words.

She discovered that the strategies she developed herself were usually the most effective ones. For her, this often incorporated her visual memory. For instance, during the early stages, she went around her house writing out the names of lots of different things in Japanese on sticky notes, and then actually sticking them on the items themselves. That way, whenever she made a cup of tea, for instance, she would be reminded of the Japanese word for *cup* and *kettle*, etc.

She also found that visualizing a scene or a journey in which she herself interacted with whatever she was learning was useful. So if she wanted to learn the word for a stapler, for instance, she would picture herself using a stapler, whilst saying the word in Japanese to herself.

Saying things out loud also helped when she was listening to films or stories. What she often did was to mimic the speaker's way of saying things, trying to replicate precisely the speaker's stress and intonation patterns. If things were said in a particularly dramatic way, this often made them more memorable for her.

It is clear that developing these strategies not only helped Angelica to remember more language, but also helped her to become a better language learner. You can hear more about her own, and others', experiences learning Japanese on a series of award-winning podcasts at http://www.soas.ac.uk/languagecentre/learners/projects/jinrikisha/

5.5 The keyword technique

Memory focus	Introducing learners to a way of making new language memorable by making connections with previously learnt words.
Level	Elementary and above
Time	20 minutes plus
Preparation	Make copies of the pictures in Box 5.5a.

Procedure

1   Give out copies of the pictures in Box 5.5a or show them on a projector. Establish with the class what they can see in each picture, focusing particularly on the following words:
    • *socket*, *sock* and *suck* for picture a)
    • *radiator*, *radio*, '*Ready?*' and '*Eat her!*' for picture b)
    • *happy*, *nappy* and *nap* for picture c)
    As well as focusing on the obvious links between these sounds, highlight the slight differences too (*suck/socket*, *ready/radiator*, *radio/radiator*, *happy/nappy*).
2   Go back through the three pictures again, asking learners to recall the words. Do they think the pictures helped them to remember the words?
3   Remove the pictures from the projector or tell the learners to turn them over. Now ask them to talk about the pictures in pairs in as much detail as they can.
4   Write the word *switch* on the board. Show them what the word means by using the light switch in the classroom. Ask the class to tell you some words they know which have similar sounds, and write them around the word. If you are working in a monolingual context, these words can be in their mother tongue. With a multilingual class or a higher-level group, it may also be possible to use English words. Some examples in English for the word *switch* could be *sweet*, *witch* and *itch*. Now ask the learners to think of an image which could link some or all of these words. Here are some examples using English:
    a light switch which you use with your tongue and it tastes really sweet
    a light switch made of a big sweet
    a witch turning on the light switch with her pointy hat
    someone scratching their itch on the light switch
    someone saying 'ssh … there's a witch' and turning off the light (using the switch) so she can't see them
    (if the learners are feeling particularly zany!) a sweet witch using the light switch to scratch her itch

5   On the board, write the names of some things that are in your classroom
     and which the learners do not already know the names for. Some
     examples might be *tiles, ceiling, projector, blinds, shutters, shelves, carpet,*
     poster, plug, window pane, window sill, protractor, curtains, etc. Check
     understanding by pointing to the objects.

6   The learners now do three things for each of the new words:
     a) Listen carefully to the teacher saying them.
     b) Think of 'help' words in L1 or L2 which sound similar.
     c) Visualize a picture which includes both the 'help' words and the
         original word.

7   Learners test each other in pairs on the English names for the items in
     the rooms. After doing this, they compare and discuss the images they
     visualized for each one. Will they be able to use this strategy for learning
     other new words in English?

Variation

Instead of using the objects in the classroom for Step 5, use the household
objects in Box 5.5b, or use another area of vocabulary more suited to the
group's needs and interests.

Box 5.5a: The keyword technique

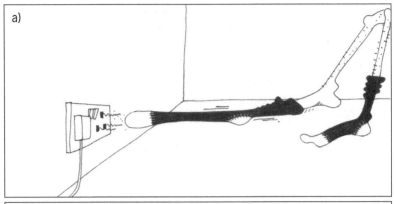

From *Memory Activities for Language Learning*
© Cambridge University Press 2011

PHOTOCOPIABLE

Box 5.5b: The keyword technique

a pair of pliers

a spatula

a screwdriver

a stapler

a drill

an Allen key

a plunger

a grater

a hacksaw

a corkscrew

From *Memory Activities for Language Learning*
© Cambridge University Press 2011   PHOTOCOPIABLE

5.6 Memory techniques survey

Memory focus	Raising awareness and sharing ideas about the different strategies used for remembering things by members of the class.
Level	Intermediate and above
Time	30 minutes plus
Preparation	Make enough copies of the question sheets in Box 5.6 so that each learner gets one (either A, B or C).

Procedure

1 Give each third of the class one of the worksheets. Ask them to go through it and make sure they understand everything.

2 Organize the class into new groups of three so that there is one person with Question sheet A, one with Question sheet B and one with Question sheet C.

3 Invite them to ask each other their questions and use this as a starting point for a discussion about memory and remembering things.

4 Learners go back to where they were originally sitting and share with the others around them what they found out.

5 Each group reports on what they have been discussing to the whole class. Try to draw out some useful conclusions and tips to go on the board.

Box 5.6: Memory techniques survey

Question sheet A

1 How good do you think you are at remembering new things in a foreign language? Poor/OK/Good/Excellent?

2 Do you think you do more remembering during class time or outside the classroom?

3 Which is harder to remember? New areas of grammar? New vocabulary? Pronunciation? Spelling? Why?

4 What makes things easy to remember? Why?

5 What do you do to help you remember things in the new language? Do you have any special techniques? What are they?

continued

Box 5.6: (*cont.*)

Question sheet B

1 How good is your memory for things? Have you ever forgotten to do something that you were supposed to do? What happened?

2 What do you do to help you remember the things you have to do? Do you have any special techniques?

3 Do you find it easy to remember people's names? How do you do it?

4 What is your earliest memory? Why do you think this memory stays with you?

5 How much do you remember of what you learnt in school a long time ago? Are there some subjects that you remember more about than others?

 -

Question sheet C

1 Are there any rules that help you remember how to write things in your first language?

2 How do you remember the number of days in each month? What about the directions of North, South, East and West?

3 Have you ever been taught any rhymes to help you remember things in your first language? Can you share them?

4 Do you find it easier to remember things if somebody shows you, or if you work it out for yourself?

5 Confucias (551 to 449 BC) said on the matter of remembering things: 'Tell me and I will forget; show me and I will learn; involve me and I will understand.' Do you think this is true for learning things in another language?

From *Memory Activities for Language Learning*
© Cambridge University Press 2011   PHOTOCOPIABLE

Variations

1 Cut the questions up into individual slips. Give a set to each group of three and ask the learners to turn them over one at a time and to discuss their answers.

2 Learners work in groups to design their own questions on the topic of memory to ask other learners. They then mingle, asking their questions before reporting the results back to their original groups.

5.7 Mnemonics quiz

Memory focus	Presenting a range of mnemonics and encouraging discussion about what they might be used for.
Level	Upper intermediate and above
Time	20 minutes plus
Preparation	Make one copy of the worksheet in Box 5.7a for each learner in the class. Copy the mnemonics in Box 5.7b, cut them up into individual items and stick each one up, spaced out around the classroom walls.

Procedure

1 Divide the class into pairs or groups of three. Give each person a copy of the worksheet in Box 5.7a.
2 When they have had a chance to read through it, ask everyone to move around the room and look at each of the mnemonics on the walls. They should remain in the same groups and discuss what they think the purpose of each of the mnemonics is. They then mark this on the worksheets. They do not need to answer the questions in any particular order.
3 When everyone has finished, go through the answers together or make copies of the answer sheet (Box 5.7c) so that they can check their own work.
4 Learners discuss each of the mnemonics in their groups. Do they know any other ways of remembering these things?

Follow-up
Test the learners on whether they can recall the facts that the mnemonic encapsulated by reading out a series of statements. If the statement is correct, they write it down as it is. If it is incorrect, they should adapt what they write to make it correct. If learners work in pairs to do this, there is more chance that they will need to discuss things and activate the language of the mnemonic more. Some example sentences to read out could be:

1 There are eight colours of the rainbow. (incorrect – there are seven)
2 Only one of the continents of the world begins with the letter E. (correct – Europe)
3 Jupiter is closer to the sun than Saturn. (correct)
4 If you start a letter with 'Dear Sir', you should finish it with 'Yours sincerely'. (incorrect – you should finish it with 'Yours faithfully')

5   In England the clocks are put back an hour in the autumn. (correct)
6   November has 31 days. (incorrect – it has 30)
7   Columbus reached America in 1492. (correct)
8   There are seven countries in Central America. (correct)
9   If the sky is red when you wake up, it means that it is going to be a nice day. (incorrect – it is going to rain)

Box 5.7a: Mnemonics quiz

A mnemonic is a way to help people to remember something that might otherwise be difficult to remember. For example, if you want to remember the names of the seven continents of the world, you might use the sentence *Eat An Apple As A Nice Snack*. The first letter of each of the words in the sentence stands for one of the continents (E: Europe, A: Africa, A: Asia, A: Australasia, A: Antarctica, N: North America, S: South America).

Work in groups of two or three. On the walls around the room you will see 10 different memory techniques. Walk around the room in your group and have a look at each one. Can you decide what each one is supposed to help you remember? How does it work? Discuss this in your group and then choose from the list below, marking each number with its corresponding letter.

1   Which is left and which is right?
2   The colours of the rainbow
3   The directions of the compass
4   The order of the planets in our solar system
5   When to use 'Yours faithfully' and when to use 'Yours sincerely' when writing a letter
6   The names of the countries in Central America
7   In which direction the clocks need to be changed
8   The number of days in each month
9   A way of predicting the weather
10 When Spanish ships first reached the continent of America

From *Memory Activities for Language Learning*
© Cambridge University Press 2011   PHOTOCOPIABLE

Box 5.7b: Mnemonics quiz

a) Never eat slimy worms.

✂ ---

b) In fourteen hundred and ninety two, Columbus sailed the ocean blue.

✂ ---

c)

✂ ---

d) Roy G. Biv

✂ ---

e) Spring forward, fall back.

✂ ---

f) Red sky at night, shepherd's delight; red sky in the morning, shepherd's warning.

✂ ---

g) Great big hungry elephants nearly consumed Panama.

✂ ---

h) My very energetic mother just served us noodles.

✂ ---

i)

✂ ---

j) Never put two Ss together.

From *Memory Activities for Language Learning*
© Cambridge University Press 2011   PHOTOCOPIABLE

Box 5.7c: Mnemonics quiz

Answers

1c) The left hand is in the shape of the letter L, which stands for 'Left'.

2d) Each of the letters of the man's name **Roy G. Biv** stands for one of the colours of the rainbow (**r**ed, **o**range, **y**ellow, **g**reen, **b**lue, **i**ndigo, **v**iolet).

3a) '**N**ever **e**at **s**limy **w**orms' has the same first letters as the four points of the compass in order (**N**orth, **S**outh, **E**ast and **W**est).

4h) '**M**y **v**ery **e**nergetic **m**other **j**ust **s**erved **u**s **n**oodles' has the same first letters as the planets in our solar system in order from the sun (**M**ercury, **V**enus, **E**arth, **M**ars, **J**upiter, **S**aturn, **U**ranus, **N**eptune).

5j) We use 'Yours faithfully' to finish a letter that starts 'Dear Sir/Madam' and 'Yours sincerely' to finish a letter that begins with 'Dear Mr/Mrs X'. So we never put two Ss together because 'Sir' never goes with 'sincerely'.

6g) '**G**reat **b**ig **h**ungry **e**lephants **n**early **c**onsumed **P**anama' has the same first letters as the countries of Central America (**G**uatemala, **B**elize, **H**onduras, **E**l Salvador, **N**icaragua, **C**osta Rica, **P**anama). The shape of the seven countries also resembles an elephant's head and trunk so this is an extra aid to memory.

7e) 'Spring forward, fall back.' In spring we put the clocks forward and lose an hour of sleep, and in fall (autumn) we put them back and gain an hour.

8i) If we put our two clenched fists in front of us we can see a series of knuckles and the falls between the knuckles. If we start counting the months from the left, one for each rise and fall, all of the months which are on a knuckle have 31 days and all the others have fewer than 31.

9f) 'Red sky at night, shepherd's delight' (if you see a red sky in the evening it means that the next day will be sunny); 'red sky in the morning, shepherd's warning' (if you see a red sky in the morning, it is going to rain).

10b) In 1492 Columbus crossed the Atlantic Ocean in a sailing ship and reached America.

From *Memory Activities for Language Learning*

Some spelling mnemonics

English spelling is less predictable than the spelling of many other languages and provides a number of memory challenges to the learner. The main problems stem from the fact that different letter clusters can produce the same sound and that double consonants are often used in an apparently arbitrary fashion. On top of this, there are a number of words containing silent letters and also lots of words that are spelt differently but with the same pronunciation (homophones). Many mnemonics have been developed to help learners to overcome some of these issues. Perhaps the most famous one applies to the order of the letters 'i' and 'e' in words: *i before e, except after c*. This works in the sentence 'I received a piece of pie from a friend', but there are so many exceptions to the rule (*protein, leisure, neighbour, science, ancient* and *efficient*, to name but a few) that its usefulness is questionable.

Perhaps it is more useful to teach rules that are more specific in their application. Here is one for the issues around adding *-ing* to verbs to make present participles.

One vowel then one consonant at the end of the verb = double the consonant (*put – putting*)

One vowel then two consonants at the end of the verb = just add *-ing* (*turn – turning*)

Verb ending in one *e* = take away the *e* and add *-ing* (*come – coming*)

Two vowels and then a consonant = just add *-ing* (*look – looking*)

Though this rule has fewer exceptions, it is not particularly memorable in its format. We can make it more so by turning its essential information into a rhyme.

If it ends in one 'E'
Set it free, add I, N, G
With one vowel, then one consonant
To double it is what you want

There are also a number of mnemonics which relate to the spelling of individual words. Learners can also be encouraged to create their own, using the mother tongue if necessary. As with other kinds of mnemonics, student-created ones will often be the most memorable. Here is a selection of ready-made ones.

Believe: Don't believe a **lie**.

Separate: There was a man called **Sep**. One day his wife saw **a rat**. She said 'Quick **Sep! A Rat!**'.

Because: Big elephants can't always understand small elephants.

Wednesday: We do not eat soup day.

Necessary: Never eat chips. Eat salad sandwiches and remain young.

Rhythm: Rhythm helps you to hear music.

Together: If you get her you will be together.

Stationary/Stationery: Stationary means not moving. There's a lazy man called 'Ary' who works at the station. He never moves! Envelopes are an item of stationery.

License, practise and advise are verbs. Licence, practice and advice are nouns. You need to 'sing' when you write the verb in its -*ing* form (practising, licensing, advising).

Affect is a verb and Effect is a noun. RAVEN – Remember: Affect = Verb, Effect = Noun.

I am accessible, responsible, incredible, invisible and flexible.

Accommodation: There are two 'c's, two 'm's and an 'o' in this word. Remember it by the phrase 'comfortable chairs in a mansion that is modern'.

5.8 Memory techniques swap

Memory focus	Exploring different memory techniques for remembering a list of items, evaluating their effectiveness and encouraging reflection about the strategies used.
Level	Pre-intermediate and above
Time	30 minutes plus
Preparation	Choose two or three of the memory techniques in Boxes 5.8a to 5.8c. Make enough copies for each half of the class to have one of them (or each third if you use three).

Procedure

1   Give one half of the class the first memory technique you have chosen and the other half the other one.
2   When they have had time to read through the exercise and try it out, ask them to work with someone else from the same half of the class and compare how they did it. Can they successfully remember the complete list of items, using this technique?

3 Now reorganize the class so that everyone is working with someone who used a different memory technique. Ask the learners to show each other how they remembered the items on their lists and to teach each other the technique. Does one of the techniques seem more effective than the others?

4 Invite people to share their views with the whole class.

Box 5.8a: Memory techniques swap

Technique 1: using rhyming words

1 bun

2 shoe

3 tree

4 door

5 hive

6 sticks

7 heaven

8 gate

9 wine

10 hen

continued

Box 5.8a: (*cont.*)

1 First you need to learn the 10 helping words above. This should be quite easy since each word rhymes with the number it goes with.

2 When you have read them through a couple of times, test yourself by covering up the words and seeing how many you can remember. If you can do them all without looking, you are ready to move on to the next stage.

3 Now let's say that here's a shopping list of 10 items that you need to buy today.

1	a telephone	6	a map of Australia
2	some olive oil	7	some yoghurt
3	a new mouse for the computer	8	camera batteries
4	a bus pass	9	a train ticket to Edinburgh
5	bicycle lights	10	a monolingual dictionary

What you need to do is to imagine a picture which links the first helping word, *bun* (number 1) with the first item on the shopping list, *a telephone*. For example, you could imagine a telephone ringing and not being able to talk because your mouth is filled up with a huge bun. The second item on the list is *some olive oil*, which needs to be linked to *shoe* (number 2). For this you could picture yourself putting your foot into your shoe and finding it is full of olive oil! Yuck! Now go through and create an image for each of the items. Remember that the more personalized the image, the easier it will be to remember. For some people, silly or strange images are easier to remember too.

4 When you have created a picture for each of the 10 items, now go through them all again, bringing to mind the same image for each one.

5 Now it is time to test yourself! Cover up everything and see if you can recall each of the 10 items on the shopping list.

From *Memory Activities for Language Learning*
© Cambridge University Press 2011 PHOTOCOPIABLE

Box 5.8b: Memory techniques swap

Technique 2: using parts of the body

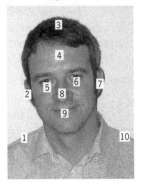

1   Look at the picture of the face above. Notice how the different parts of the body are labelled with a different number from 1 to 10. Go through them all and try to remember which number goes with which body part.

2   Now let's say that here's a shopping list of 10 items that you need to buy today.

1	a telephone	6	a map of Australia
2	some olive oil	7	some yoghurt
3	a new mouse for the computer	8	camera batteries
4	a bus pass	9	a train ticket to Edinburgh
5	bicycle lights	10	a monolingual dictionary

3   What you need to do now is to imagine a picture which links the first item, *a telephone*, with the appropriate part of your body, *your right shoulder*. For example, you could imagine that you are talking into your telephone but you cannot use your hands for some reason, so you are holding it between your chin and your right shoulder. The second item on the list is *some olive oil*, which needs to be linked to *your right ear* (number 2). For this you could imagine somebody pouring olive oil into your ear to make the wax inside go soft. Now go through and create an image for each of the numbers. Remember that the more personalized the image, the easier it will be to remember. For some people, silly or strange images are easier to remember too.

4   When you have created a picture for each of the 10 items, go through them all again, bringing to mind the same image for each one as you look at the face.

5   Now it is time to test yourself! Cover up everything and see if you can recall each of the 10 items on the shopping list.

From *Memory Activities for Language Learning*
PHOTOCOPIABLE

Box 5.8c: Memory techniques swap

Technique 3: using acronyms

1   Imagine that this is a shopping list of 10 items that you need to buy today. What you're going to do is to try to remember all of these items without looking at the list.

1	a **t**elephone	6	a map of **A**ustralia
2	some **o**live oil	7	some **y**oghurt
3	a new **m**ouse for the computer	8	camera **b**atteries
4	a bus **p**ass	9	a train ticket to **E**dinburgh
5	bicycle **l**ights	10	a monolingual **d**ictionary

2   You will notice that each of the items has a letter in it which has been highlighted. If you write out all of these letters in order, it will spell TOM PLAY BED. Remembering these words should be much easier than remembering the whole list. Say it to yourself a few times. You can probably remember it already.

3   Now go through the list above, noticing and trying to remember what each of the letters stands for. So T stands for *telephone*, O stands for *olive oil*, etc.

4   When you have done this a couple of times, it is time to give yourself a test. Without looking at the list, try to remember what is on it just by going through the letters of TOM PLAY BED.

5   Do not worry if you cannot remember all of them straightaway. Go back to the list and remind yourself of the ones you didn't remember. Keep repeating this process until you feel you can remember everything.

From *Memory Activities for Language Learning*

5.9 Memory techniques activation

Memory focus	Choosing a memory technique and using it to recall a learner-generated list of items on a shopping list. Storing and retrieving items from a shopping list.
Level	Pre-intermediate and above
Time	20 minutes plus
Preparation	This activity works as a follow-up to Activity 5.8: *Memory techniques swap.*

Procedure

1 Ask the learners to write their own shopping list of 10 items. These should be items that they really want or need at that moment, and that could be bought from a variety of different places. Make dictionaries available, and help out with vocabulary if required.

2 When they have finished their lists, ask them to discuss in pairs what would be the best way for them to remember the items. This could be using the technique that they used in Activity 5.8, using the one that their partner used or something entirely different of their own choosing.

3 Allow plenty of time for them to try to recall their items and to test themselves.

4 When they feel they are ready, ask the learners to swap lists with the person next to them and to try to 'buy' the items from their lists from memory. The partner takes on the role of the shop assistant (in a shop that sells everything!) and may ask questions to find out more about what exactly is required. For example: *Do you want a birthday cake? Is it for a child or an adult? Do you want candles with it?* and so on.

5 Learners give each other feedback on how well they remembered the items on their lists.

5.10 Acronyms for grammatical patterns

Memory focus	Making grammatical patterns memorable using acronyms.
Level	Pre-intermediate and above
Time	15 minutes plus
Preparation	None

Procedure

1 Write the names of some or all of the people in Box 5.10a on the board (without what is written in brackets). Tell the class that they are the names of some people who share a house together and that one day they decided to have a party. Each of the people had different ideas about what kind of party to have and how it should be organized.

2 Go through each of the names explaining what each person did. To make it clear that the letters of the surname are an acronym for the verb phrase, point at each letter of the surname in turn as you say each word. After saying each name, ask somebody to repeat back to you what the person did.

3 Now ask them to go through all of the names in pairs. Can they remember what each person did just by looking at the names on the board? Be available to prompt them where necessary.

4 You can gradually increase the level of challenge by removing more and more of what is written on the board. Can they remember the surnames as well as the verb phrases just by looking at the first names? Eventually clear the board completely and ask the learners to recall as many of the complete names as they can, as well as what each person did.

Box 5.10a: Acronyms for grammatical patterns

Diana D. THAP (decided to have a party)

Wendy WETHARNT (wanted everyone to have a really nice time)

Leo LEBACOF (let everyone bring a couple of friends)

Ian ITNAW (invited the neighbours as well)

Terry TETWAC (told everyone to wear a costume)

Wally WABEF (was annoyed because everyone forgot)

Edward EGER (enjoyed getting everything ready)

Barbara BLONT-TEAD (bought lots of nice things to eat and drink)

Penny PSYCO (prepared some yummy cheese omelettes)

Graham GRUBEAL (got really upset because everyone arrived late)

Mary METTSO (made everyone take their shoes off)

Amanda ATGITWAD (asked the guests if they wanted a drink)

Tina TUTHA (tidied up the house afterwards)

From *Memory Activities for Language Learning*
© Cambridge University Press 2011   PHOTOCOPIABLE

Variation

Acronyms are also a useful tool for memorizing a range of other grammatical structures. For instance, to remember the order of elements in a question, we can use the acronym WASV (W = Wh word, A = Auxiliary, S = Subject, V = Verb) in questions like *Where do you work? Are you leaving?* etc. Box 5.10b provides some further examples focusing on common English tenses. These can be incorporated into a language presentation stage on the board, and then used as an aid to recall the example sentence later.

Box 5.10b: Acronyms for grammatical patterns

DAWN	*Does anyone want nuts?* (present simple question form)
WAY DOWN	*What are you doing on Wednesday night?* (present continuous question form)
DEARLY	*Did everyone arrive really late yesterday?* (past simple question form)
WOW WOW	*Was Oscar wearing waterproofs on Wednesday?* (past continuous question form)
HASTE	*Has anyone seen* The Exorcist */ the eggs?* (present perfect question form)
WHY BE?	*What have you been eating?* (present perfect continuous question form)
WHAT'S HEAT BATH?	*When Helen arrived there she hadn't expected anyone to be at the house.* (past perfect)
SHABAFTY WHEATS	*Stallone had already been acting for ten years when he enrolled at theatre school.* (past perfect continuous)
WW BB TT	*Who will Beatriz be teaching tomorrow?* (future continuous question form)
BE A NEW HIM	*By early August, Nikolai's English will have improved massively.* (future perfect)

From *Memory Activities for Language Learning*
© Cambridge University Press 2011   PHOTOCOPIABLE

For more examples of using acronyms to make grammatical forms memorable, see Simon Mumford's excellent article in *Humanising Language Teaching* at http://www.hltmag.co.uk/dec08/mart03.htm

Acronyms for internet passwords

If learners use the internet to buy things, to check the balance on their bank accounts, or to post on online social networking sites and discussion groups, the chances are that they will be using passwords to log in to many of these sites. In order to prevent internet fraud, it is advisable to use different passwords for each different site, and also to choose passwords which are sufficiently difficult to guess. Here's a neat way to construct a complicated password that will always be remembered, and which will review their grammar at the same time. Learners choose an area of grammar which is new for them, or which they're struggling to remember how to construct. They then write a sentence which applies to their own lives, using the form, and check that it's correct with someone they trust. For instance they might write:

I've been living in Porto Alegre since July '93.

They then reduce the sentence to an acronym like this:

iblipasj93

They can now use this as a password for one of their online activities. Each time they use that service, they will be providing themselves with a quick review of the form, and since it doesn't contain any full words, it will be impossible to guess by anyone attempting to access the account illegally.

6   Learning by heart

When I was young I had a dream,
To watch the greatest football team,
And here I am, the dream is real,
With Randy Lerner and Martin O'Neill ...
Martin O'Neill, Martin O'Neill, Martin O'Neill,
      Martin O'Neill ...

On a good day, the above text may have been chanted over and over again simultaneously by hundreds, possibly thousands, of enthusiastic fans when Martin O'Neill was manager of Aston Villa Football Club. It was not, of course, handed out to the supporters on pieces of paper for them to read from, but instead, along with the many other chants which may be known by the supporters of a particular team, it was learnt entirely by heart. This process is made possible by the fact that many of the mnemonic devices that have been explored in previous chapters, such as rhyme, rhythm, repetition and gesture, have been deliberately woven into both its internal structure and the way it is performed.

Before the advent of writing, committing entire spoken texts to memory like this, both for personal processing and for passing down information to future generations, was the only way in which certain bodies of knowledge could be retained. Because of this, mnemonic features were often present in religious texts, in stories and in poems, and the ability to learn such texts by heart was a basic requirement, particularly for teachers and learners, but also for society in general. The following breakfast chant (in its original Pali with a translation on the right) dates back as far as 15 centuries ago and spread throughout much of the Buddhist world. It would have been learnt and recited before eating each morning.

sabba-roga-vinimutto,	May you be free from all sickness,
sabba-santāpa-vajjito;	May you be free from all troubles;
sabba-veram-atikkanto,	Passing beyond all enmity,
nibbuto ca tuvam-bhava;	May you attain liberation;
sabb'ītiyo vivajjantu,	May you be free from all bad things,
sabba-rogo vinassatu;	May all of your sickness be cured;

māte bhavatv-antarāyo,	May you never be faced by danger,
sukhī dīgh'āyuko bhava.	May you be happy and live long.

Of course, meal chants are still memorized and passed on orally today. One of the few texts of any kind that I can still remember from the time I was at primary school was the much more direct *For what we are about to receive, may the Lord make us truly thankful. Amen*, which we were made to say before our school dinners could be attacked.

With the increase in availability of written texts and the spread of world literacy over the last few decades, it has become pertinent to ask whether there is any need to learn texts if we can find them easily in books or even write them down ourselves. Today, as we move deeper and deeper into the digital age, where copious amounts of information can be accessed with just a few clicks of the mouse, the need to remember things precisely seems to be becoming even less important. In fact, more and more of the workload of memorizing information has been delegated to other places; from within our own minds, to written texts, to our computer hard drives, and now to the internet itself.

So is learning a text by heart still a valid learning activity? Despite being viewed in some circles as outdated and uncommunicative, it is still widely used in many diverse educational settings. It is common practice in many Islamic schools around the world, for instance, for learners of all ages to commit large sections, and sometimes all, of the Koran to memory. Although the methods used in some centres have been criticized for being unnecessarily harsh, and it is not always clear that those doing the learning actually understand what they are memorizing, it has also been suggested that the huge bank of language that gets built up in long-term memory as a result of this process is a fantastic resource to draw on for more creative output later. In fact, many of the greatest writers in the Arabic language have gone through the experience of memorizing large parts of the Koran at some point in their lives.

Learning by heart is also popular in secular contexts such as China, where memorization of material has traditionally been emphasized over creative use of language. Research by Yanren Ding (2007) has shown that highly successful language learners, who perform very well in national competitions in speaking and debating in English, will often regard their previous experiences of learning texts by heart as the single most important factor in their language development.

What these examples show is that perhaps there is more to learning by heart than purely remembering the content of the text to be learnt. It seems that it can also play a role in developing awareness about the language areas that the text contains. Many researchers now suggest that we are much less original when using language than was previously thought, relying instead, to a large extent, on the store of chunks, fixed expressions and other formulaic language items that have already been added to our mental lexicons. If this is the case, then memorizing texts that are rich in such patterns makes sense, providing of course that the meanings are fully understood by the learners and that the content is appropriate to their needs and interests. It helps too, of course, if the learners are personally involved in choosing or shaping the material to be learnt, and this is something which should be addressed as far as possible with the activities that follow.

It is also important to bear in mind that learning material by heart as a language-learning activity can be a highly contentious issue. Learners as well as teachers sometimes have strong views about its effectiveness, and this is often based on their previous learning experiences. This discussion should be encouraged as much as possible as a way of reflecting on the activities and of raising awareness about the preferred learning styles of others.

6.1 Co-constructed conversation

Memory focus	Committing a learner-generated conversation to memory.
Level	Beginner and above
Time	20 minutes
Preparation	Find an interesting picture that shows people interacting in some way (see the example in Box 6.1). You will also need some way of recording speech.

Procedure

1 Give out copies of the picture or show it on a projector. Elicit some ideas about what the people might be saying. If working with a low-level group, this could happen in the mother tongue (L1).
2 Ask for volunteers or choose some people to take on the roles of the characters in the picture. Ask them to come to the front of the class and to organize themselves in such a way that they imitate the picture as much as possible.

3   Elicit from the class, in L1 if necessary, what they think the first thing to be said in the situation might be. If necessary, elicit or supply a more accurate or appropriate version of this (or a translation if it came in L1). Practise the utterance several times with the person 'in the picture' until he or she feels comfortable with it, and then ask him or her to record it. You now have the first line of the conversation.

4   Now ask for suggestions as to how the other person could respond to this. Keep repeating the procedure of modelling the utterance yourself, practising it with the appropriate person, and then asking him or her to record it. Continue this process until you have built up a recording of about 10 lines of dialogue.

5   Now play the recording back to the class. Pause after each utterance and elicit which character said it. (If working in a monolingual context, you can also elicit an L1 translation here.)

6   Now play it again, this time eliciting the English version of each line before it comes up on the recording, and then transcribing it onto the board.

7   The conversation on the board can now be used for some language analysis work. Check that the learners understand some of the individual parts of the utterances. Rub out some of the words. Can they remember what the missing words are? Try gradually rubbing out more and more of the conversation while continuing to ask the class to remember what is missing. Keep going until you have managed to rub out the entire conversation.

8   Put the learners into groups and ask them to practise the conversation as naturally as possible from memory.

Box 6.1: Co-constructed conversation

From *Memory Activities for Language Learning* © Cambridge University Press 2011

PHOTOCOPIABLE

6.2 Blocking a dialogue

Memory focus	Learning a short dialogue by heart and helping to automatize the language it contains.
Level	Pre-intermediate and above
Time	30 minutes plus
Preparation	Find a short dialogue from a play or film that contains language appropriate to the level of the group and that can easily be split into two parts. (See the example in Box 6.2 from David Lynch's film *Mulholland Drive* for a class at pre-intermediate level or above.) If you have internet access, then try to find a video extract of the scene to play as a follow-up. Several versions of the example used here can be found by searching for 'mulholland drive audition' at a site like YouTube™ (http://www.youtube.com/).

Procedure

1   Give one part of the scene to one half of the class and the other part to the other half (Box 6.2).
2   In groups of three, the learners work through the following tasks. It may help to write these tasks on the board:
    • Read through the dialogue together and make sure you understand it. Where do you think the characters are? Who are they? What is the relationship between them?
    • Choose two people to play the two characters (A and B). The other person acts as 'director'.
    • Bring the dialogue to life by adding gestures and movements. Try to find something to go with each line. The director watches the scene and makes suggestions.
    • Once you have done the dialogue a few times with the text, try doing it from memory without looking. The director can help by giving the first word or two of a line if somebody forgets something.
    • Keep practising the dialogue until you feel comfortable with the lines and the movements.
3   Now put one pair from one side of the class with another pair from the other side. Ask them to perform their dialogues to each other and to comment on them.
4   Ask for volunteers to perform their versions in front of the whole class.
5   Now play the recording of the whole scene to the class (if available). What differences do they notice between this one and their own interpretations?

Box 6.2: Blocking a dialogue

Part 1

A: You're still here?

B: I came back. I thought that's what you wanted.

A: Nobody wants you here!

B: Really?

A: My parents are right upstairs! They think you've left.

B: So ... surprise ...

A: I can call them ... I can call my dad ...

B: But you won't ...

A: You're playing a dangerous game here. If you're trying to blackmail me ... it's not going to work.

Part 2

B: You know what I want ... it's not that difficult.

A: Get out! Get out before I call my dad ... he trusts you ... you're his best friend. This will be the end of everything.

B: What about you? What will your dad think about you?

A: Stop it! That's what you said from the beginning. If I tell them what happened, they'll arrest you and put you in jail, so get out of here before ...

B: Before what?

A: Before I kill you.

B: Well, then they'd put you in jail.

A: I hate you. I hate us both.

© David Lynch

From *Memory Activities for Language Learning*
© Cambridge University Press 2011   PHOTOCOPIABLE

How do actors remember their lines?

You must be able to stand there, not thinking of that line. You take it off the other actor's face. (Michael Caine, British actor, born 1933)

Actors, both those who work professionally and those who do it on an amateur basis, are one kind of people who are often very experienced and skilled in learning material by heart. Here are some of the strategies and techniques that they use, all of which may have implications for the learning of text in the language class.

- *Sensory channels*: The more the senses can be brought into play when memorizing, the better. For many actors, saying their lines out loud is more beneficial than simply reading them, and some people find that copying them out can also help. Others find that recording their own and/ or the other characters' words and then playing them back can be useful.
- *Gestures and physicalization*: Noice and Noice's (2006) research found that using movements and physical gestures that were appropriate to the meaning of the line at the time of memorization really helped the line to stick. Interestingly, it was not always necessary to retrieve the movement in order to retrieve the corresponding line.
- *Personalization and emotional investment*: If actors can identify with what the character is saying and relate it in some way to their own experiences and lives, this can make the lines more memorable. Similarly, getting to grips with the emotional content and really feeling what is being expressed will also help.
- *Beats*: Often long passages are broken up by actors into single units of meaning called beats. Each beat will be memorized as a whole by linking it to a particular intention, emotion or movement.
- *Cues*: Learning dialogue with another person is often easier than alone. If we remember the last part of the lines before our own, this can serve as a cue to remind us of what to say ourselves.
- *Prompts*: Having a non-acting assistant who can supply a hint when we forget a line can be very useful. These hints should provide enough of the words to serve as a memory trigger, but not so much that the retrieval process is taken away from the actor.
- *Testing*: Some actors cover the text with a piece of paper and then recite their lines, slowly revealing the text to check whether they were correct. Believing that you know the lines, and therefore trying to practise the text without looking, is often more beneficial than simply reading the text again and again.

6.3 Songs

Memory focus	Learning the words of a short song by heart, and providing an input flood of an area of language (conditional sentences are used in the example in Box 6.3a).
Level	Pre-intermediate and above
Time	15 minutes
Preparation	Each pair or small group needs a set of rhyming song lyrics which have been cut up into strips (see the example in Box 6.3a).

Procedure

1 Give out a set of the cut-up slips to each pair or small group of learners. Tell them that there is a rhyme running all the way through the song between the last syllable of one line, and the last syllable of the next one (giving an example if necessary). Ask them to put the slips into a logical order so that this rhyming pattern is continued throughout.
2 When you've checked that everyone has the correct order, ask each pair to turn over all of the even-numbered lines (2, 4, 6, etc.). In their pairs, can they remember what each missing line says? They turn over to check once they have had a go.
3 They can now turn over the odd-numbered lines and repeat the procedure. Eventually ask them to turn over all of the lines. Can they now remember the complete song?
4 Play the song for them and/or sing it with them.

Variation

The site http://www.memorizenow.com/ allows learners to paste in the lyrics of a song, or any other text for that matter. It then creates a variety of memory exercises to help with learning the text by heart.

Notes

See Box 6.3b for a more modern interpretation of this traditional song. The lyrics for these songs also work well as chant, with half the class chanting the lines beginning *If that …* and the other half responding with *Mama's going to buy you …* or *'Cause/Then I'm gonna buy you … .*

Box 6.3a: Songs

Hush little baby, don't say a word

✂---

Mama's going to buy you a mocking bird
If that mocking bird won't sing

✂---

Mama's going to buy you a diamond ring
If that diamond ring turns to brass

✂---

Mama's going to buy you a looking glass
If that looking glass gets broke

✂---

Mama's going to buy you a billy goat
If that billy goat won't pull

✂---

Mama's going to buy you a cart and bull
If that cart and bull turns over

✂---

Mama's going to buy you a dog named Rover
If that dog named Rover won't bark

✂---

Mama's going to buy you a horse and cart
If that horse and cart breaks down

✂---

You'll still be the sweetest little baby in town
So hush little baby, don't you cry

✂---

Daddy loves you and so do I

Box 6.3b: Songs

Hush now my darling, don't say a word

✂--

'Cause I'm gonna buy you a singing bird
If that singing bird won't sing

✂--

Then I'm gonna buy you a diamond ring
If that diamond ring won't shine

✂--

Then I'm gonna buy you a bottle of wine
If that bottle of wine gets cracked

✂--

Then I'm gonna buy you a Cadillac
If that Cadillac won't start

✂--

Then I'm gonna buy you an apple tart
If that apple tart tastes sour

✂--

Then I'm gonna buy you a power shower
If that power shower starts to hurt

✂--

Then I'm gonna buy you a linen shirt
If that linen shirt won't fit

✂--

Then I'm gonna say 'Oh sugar — I quit!'

From *Memory Activities for Language Learning*

6.4 Puns

Memory focus	Learning a pun by heart and making language memorable through exploring humour and double meanings.
Level	Pre-intermediate and above (depending on the puns chosen)
Time	30 minutes plus
Preparation	Each group of two to four learners will need a copy of a short pun. See the examples in Box 6.4. (NB These puns should be used at the teacher's discretion and it is very important to be mindful of the cultural sensitivities of your class at all times.)

Procedure

1   Give each pair or small group of learners a different pun to work with. Ask them to consult other people or dictionaries if there are any meanings they are unsure about. All of the puns in Box 6.4 work around the double meanings of words, so the key to understanding the pun is to understand what these two meanings are.
2   Ask them to memorize it exactly so that they could tell it to somebody else without looking at the text.
3   Now ask everyone to mingle and tell their puns to people from other groups. If someone does not understand a pun, the teller should make things clear by explaining the double meanings.
4   Everyone sits down again and shares the puns that they heard with the other members of their group.

Follow-up
At Step 4 each group compiles a list of all of the puns that they can remember.

Box 6.4: Puns

1 Two aerials got married. The wedding was pretty bad, but the reception was great.

2 One thousand pairs of underpants have been stolen. The police are making a brief enquiry.

3 Did you hear about the man who lost the whole left side of his body? He's all right now.

4 What is the prisoner's favourite punctuation mark? The full stop – it marks the end of his sentence.

5 The police have caught two men drinking battery acid. They will soon be charged.

6 Why did the man give up tap dancing? Because he kept falling in the sink.

7 Did you hear about the fire on the campsite? The heat was in tents.

8 Why is it a problem if you get sick at the airport? It could be a terminal illness.

9 A young pilot flew through a rainbow during his test. He passed with flying colours.

10 Why are Italians so good at making coffee? Because they really know how to espresso themselves.

11 Two peanuts were walking in a very tough area. One of them was a salted.

12 What happened to the pupil who missed school to go bungee jumping? He ended up getting suspended.

13 What happened to the thief who got his leg stuck in wet cement? He became a hardened criminal.

14 Two hospitals are working together to develop artificial arms and legs. It's a joint project.

15 Why are pilots so successful? Because they've got friends in high places.

16 What happened when the two pencils decided to have a race? It ended in a draw.

17 Why is it so wet in England? Because the queen has been reigning for a very long time.

6.5 News stories

Memory focus	Learning a short news story by heart
Level	Intermediate and above
Time	Homework task (10 minutes in class)
Preparation	Choose two or more short news stories of around 100 words, which your class may find interesting and which are at an appropriate level. A wide range of short stories can be found at http://web.orange.co.uk/p/news/home/ See the examples in Box 6.5a. Give half of the class one of the stories, and the other half another. Ask everyone to check any meanings they are unsure about and to memorize the story word for word for homework. They need to get to a level where they can repeat it in the next class without looking at the text.

Procedure

1 Ask students to form pairs with someone who learnt the same text as they did for homework.

2 Ask them to prompt each other in their pairs: one person tries to recall the text without looking, while the other looks at the text and helps out by saying the next word where necessary.

3 Now mix learners up so that they are working with someone with a different text. Ask them to swap texts and repeat the process. Again the listener acts as a prompt where necessary.

4 When they have done this, learners discuss the texts they have worked with in their new pairs. Do they identify with the people? Could the events happen in other cultures that the learners know?

5 Now ask learners to reflect on the process of text memorization that they went through. Were there some parts that were easier than others to memorize? Did they feel it was a useful thing to do for their own language development?

Variations

1 If learners have internet access outside the class, they can be asked to find their own short stories to memorize. In this way a greater range of stories may be possible, and it is also likely that learners will encounter fewer difficulties in memorizing a text they have chosen themselves.

2   At some stage in the memorization process, learners can use a hint sheet for the text (see an example in Box 6.5b). This is a good way for them to make sure that they are remembering to include all the small words like articles and prepositions.

Follow-up

The memorized stories can be performed as a newscast and videoed for use in subsequent lessons, or to show to other learners.

Box 6.5a: News stories

Story A

The Irish police force has finally solved the mystery of the Polish driver, Prawo Jazdy, who was guilty of over 50 separate driving offences in various locations all over the country. The offender had always provided different addresses and had never been caught. With the help of a Polish–English dictionary, police discovered that Prawo Jazdy, which is printed in the top right-hand corner of every licence, actually means 'driving licence' in Polish, rather than being the name of the holder. If nothing else has been learnt from this incident, Irish police officers now know at least two words in Polish.

Story B

A Japanese man has taken the unusual step of marrying his virtual girlfriend in a very bizarre wedding ceremony, attended by a priest, a DJ, and friends and family. His new wife, Nene Anegasaki, is a fictional character in a Nintendo game, 'Love Plus', of which he is a big fan. Players are invited to choose a partner and then take her on dates, buy her flowers and perform other 'boyfriend duties'. So far this is the first time anyone has taken such a relationship into the real world. 'The two of us hope to continue to let our love for each other grow as time goes on,' he said.

From *Memory Activities for Language Learning*
© Cambridge University Press 2011   PHOTOCOPIABLE

> ## Box 6.5b: News stories
>
> ### Story A
>
> T–l–p–f–h–f–s–t–m–o–t–P–d, P–J, w–w–g–o–o–50–s–d–o–
> i–v–l–a–o–t–c. T–o–h–a–p–d–a–a–h–n–b–c. W–t–h–o–a–P–
> E–d, p–d–t–P–J, w–i–p–i–t–t–r-h–c–o–e–l, a–m–'d–l'–i–P, r–t–
> b–t–n–o–t–h. l–n–e–h–b–l–f–t–i, l–p–o–n–k–a–l–2–w–i–P.
>
> --
>
> ### Story B
>
> A–J–m–h–t–t–u–s–o–m–h–ṽ–g–i–a–v–b–w–c, a–b–a–p, a–
> DJ, a–f–a–f. H–n–w, N–A, i–a–f–c–i–a–N–g, 'L–P', o–w–h–i–a–
> b–f. P–a–i–t–c–a–p–a–t–t–h–o–d, b–h–f–a–p–o–'b–d'. S–f–
> t–i–t–f–t–a–h–t–s–a–r–i–t–r–w. 'T–t–o–u–h–t–c–t–l–o–l–
> f–e–o–g–a–t–g–o,' h–s.
>

Francisco's story

In 1987, at the height of Angola's long and bloody civil war, a young
Angolan man called Francisco Matete stepped off the plane to start his
new life in Moscow. Like many of his fellow countrymen, under the terms
of the special relationship between the Angolan government and the Soviet
Union, he had taken up the offer of a full scholarship to study at a Russian
university.

After doing a year's foundation course in Russian, he began studying
engineering but quickly found that it was in the area of languages where
his real interests lay. He moved to Minsk, eventually doing an MA in
English Linguistics and Translation. The course focused principally on
language development, but contained very few of the features of what
could be referred to as a communicative syllabus. There were no role plays,
no information-gap activities, no debates and discussions, in fact very little
focus on using language for communication at all! And yet Francisco's
English ability soared.

By the end of the course, he had accumulated a vast vocabulary and a sound grammatical awareness. He was generally able to work out the pronunciation of a new word just by reading it, and, despite never having been to the United Kingdom, or having to use English to communicate with British people, he had acquired a very 'English' way of speaking.

How was this possible? Francisco attributes his success as a learner of English to one principal factor: the memorization of texts. In each class the students on the course would be shown poems, extracts of prose or dialogues, which they would be asked to memorize. They would then be left in the language laboratory to listen to the texts again and again, and to practise them until they felt comfortable that they had learnt both the words and the correct pronunciation patterns. In the next class, each student would have to recite the text aloud without looking at the original.

At the time of writing, many years after completing his MA, Francisco teaches English at an Angolan university and is the president of the Angolan English teachers association (ANELTA). What is interesting is that he is still able to recite many of the texts that he memorized all those years ago. Learning by heart has played a huge part in his own language development and now informs to a large extent his own approach to language teaching.

6.6 Poems

Memory focus	Learning a poem by heart.
Level	Elementary and above
Time	20 minutes plus (depending on the class size)
Preparation	Find some short poems which are appropriate to the level of the learners. Many can be found on the internet by typing 'short poem' or 'limericks' into a search engine like Google (http://www.google.com/). The limericks in Box 6.6 are suitable for an upper intermediate or advanced group. (NB The content of limericks is often of a bawdy and humorous nature. Teachers should be mindful at all times of the cultural sensitivities of learners when deciding whether to use such material.)

Procedure

1 Use one of the poems as an example, and write it out on the board. Go through it with the class, modelling the rhythm (if it has one) and using paraphrases or translation to make sure everyone is aware of meanings. Allow everyone plenty of practice so that they can say the poem naturally themselves.

2 Give a different poem to individual learners, or to pairs or small groups. Ask them to check the meanings of unfamiliar vocabulary by consulting dictionaries, each other or the teacher. They then learn it by heart so that they can perform it without looking at the text.

3 Learners perform their poems for everyone else. If they are working in pairs or groups, it may be more appropriate for them to divide up the lines between them. With a very large class, mix learners up so that people from different groups are working together for the performance stage.

Variation
Encourage learners to find their own poems to learn by heart for homework.

Box 6.6: Poems

There once was a young girl from Crewe,
Who dreamed she was eating her shoe;
She woke up in the night
With a terrible fright
And found it was perfectly true.

A glutton who came from the Rhine,
When asked at what hour he would dine,
Replied, 'At eleven,
At three, five, and seven,
At eight, and a quarter past nine.'

There once was an old man of Esser,
Whose knowledge grew lesser and lesser;
It at last grew so small,
He knew nothing at all,
And now he's a college professor.

There was a young girl from New York,
Whose body was lighter than cork;
She had to be fed
On pieces of lead
Before she went out for a walk.

There was an old man of Khartoum,
Who kept a tame sheep in his room;
'To remind me,' he said,
'Of someone who's dead,
But I never can recollect whom.'

There was a young lady from Hyde,
Who ate thirty apples, then died;
While her lover lamented,
The apples fermented,
Now there's cider inside her inside.

There once was a man of Bengal,
Who was asked to a fancy-dress ball;
He said, 'I will risk it
And go as a biscuit'
But a dog ate him up in the hall.

A man from the Isle of Wight
Could travel much faster than light.
He set off one day,
In the usual way,
And returned on the previous night.

✂

From *Memory Activities for Language Learning*
© Cambridge University Press 2011

6.7 Quotations

Memory focus	Learning famous people quotations by heart.
Level	Upper intermediate and above
Time	10 minutes plus (depending on the number of students)
Preparation	For homework ask learners to search for quotations by famous people using a search engine like Google™ (http://www.google.com/) or to go to a quotations website like http://www.quotationspage.com/ On this site quotations can be searched for by keyword, theme or author and there is a huge range of quotes by famous people. The learners' task is to choose a quotation and to memorize it exactly. The author should be someone whose name will be known by everyone in the class. If internet access is not available, then choose some quotations from Box 6.7.

Procedure

1   In the next class each learner gives you the name of the person they are quoting on a small piece of paper. Write them up in a random order on the board.

2   Ask each learner to say the quotation they have memorized to the rest of the class, without saying the name of the person. If working in a monolingual class, it may also be appropriate for the learners to follow up the quotation with their own translation of it into their mother tongue. The other people in the class write down the name of the famous person who they think said the quotation next to the name of the learner who said it in class.

3   When everyone has spoken, go through all the answers together. Award a prize for the person who has the most correct answers.

Box 6.7: Quotations

1   *It takes a great deal of courage to stand up to your enemies, but even more to stand up to your friends.* (J. K. Rowling, British author, born 1965)

2   *There is nothing like returning to a place that remains unchanged to find the ways in which you yourself have altered.* (Nelson Mandela, former President of South Africa, born 1918)

3   *I usually make up my mind about a man in ten seconds; and I very rarely change it.* (Margaret Thatcher, former British Prime Minister, born 1925)

4   *The ultimate measure of a man is not where he stands in moments of comfort and convenience, but where he stands at times of challenge and controversy.* (Martin Luther King, Jr, American civil rights leader, born 1929)

5   *Happiness is when what you think, what you say, and what you do are in harmony.* (Mahatma Gandhi, Indian political and spiritual leader, born 1869)

6   *The more laws and order are made prominent, the more thieves and robbers there will be.* (Lao-tzu, Chinese philosopher, born 604 BC)

7   *Wise men talk because they have something to say; fools, because they have to say something.* (Plato, Greek philosopher, born 427 BC)

8   *If you want to make peace, you don't talk to your friends. You talk to your enemies.* (Moshe Dayan, Israeli general and politician, born 1915)

9   *Always forgive your enemies; nothing annoys them so much.* (Oscar Wilde, Irish dramatist, novelist and poet, born 1854)

10 *I pay no attention whatever to anybody's praise or blame. I simply follow my own feelings.* (Wolfgang Amadeus Mozart, Austrian composer, born 1756)

11 *Success is a lousy teacher. It seduces smart people into thinking they can't lose.* (Bill Gates, American software designer, born 1955)

12 *We are here because we love this country too much to let the next four years look like the last eight.* (Barack Obama, 44th President of the United States, born 1961)

13 *If you enter this world knowing you are loved and you leave this world knowing the same, then everything that happens in between can be dealt with.* (Michael Jackson, American singer, born 1958)

14 *I have come to accept that if I have a new haircut it is front-page news. But having a picture of my foot on the front page of a national newspaper is a bit exceptional.* (David Beckham, British footballer, born 1975)

From *Memory Activities for Language Learning*
© Cambridge University Press 2011   PHOTOCOPIABLE

Follow-up
Ask learners to work in pairs and go through all the names on the board again. How many quotations can they remember the gist of?

Variations
1 Instead of using quotations, ask the learners to remember part of the lyrics of a pop song by a well-known band. As above, the names of the bands are written on the board and other learners have to guess which band's song they belong to. The lyrics for many pop songs can be found by typing the song title and the word 'lyrics' into an internet search engine.
2 Ask pairs to choose a short film that they both like with its film script available on the internet. (Search for the film title and the word 'script'). They choose a very short dialogue from the film script to learn by heart. The film titles are written on the board in the next class and the procedure continues as above.

6.8 The sample answer recall game

Memory focus	Playing a game in which sections of a sample answer for a writing exam are learnt by heart.
Level	Intermediate and above
Time	20 minutes plus (depending on the length of the sample answer)
Preparation	Find a sample answer for a writing exam which is at the level of the class. See the example in Box 6.8 for a group at upper intermediate level and above. This text has been adapted from a sample answer written by Emma Lay from Aston University.

Procedure

1 Organize the class into groups of four or five. Display the sample answer on a projector, or give out copies.
2 The learners' task as a group is to memorize exactly as much of the text as possible. Ask each group to divide the text up between them so that each person gets roughly an equal share.
3 Each group now takes it in turn to send a person to the front of the class. Facing the front, so that he or she cannot see the text, this person now has to recite the section of the text that he or she has memorized. The members of other groups listen and award points at the end based on how many words were correctly memorized.

Note
This activity was suggested by Tiffany Key, a teacher of English in Japan.

Variation
Allow learners to choose their own texts to memorize for homework. These could be dialogues or short texts from their coursebook, or poems or extracts of prose that they find on the internet. Points can be awarded according to level of difficulty, delivery and length of text.

Box 6.8: The sample answer recall game

Technology and its constant developments have had a profound influence on the world in which we live. As internet use has increased, the world has become a smaller place, and the ways in which we communicate with each other have become more varied. There are those who claim that this high-tech society has made us forget what is important in life, namely family and friends. In my opinion, there have been both benefits and drawbacks to technological advances for social relationships, and this essay will deal with them in two sections: the positive influences of technology and the negative.

In terms of the advantageous effects technology has had on our social lives, we could put forward the case of chat rooms and online forums. These two phenomena have seen amazing growth in the world of cyberspace. People can now meet and forge friendships worldwide, and those who live in isolated locations are now able to build relationships and exchange experiences and ideas that, without the internet, they would not previously have been able to do. This is one way in which technology has brought people together rather than distanced them.

However, when considering technology, we can also identify its negative impact on social relationships. A case in point is that physical contact between people seems to have seriously diminished with the advent of mobile phones. Nowadays children who possess mobiles may call and text their friends (even those who live next door) rather than going to visit them in person. This disintegration of social contact surely affects a child's social skills and ability to interact with people on a personal basis.

This alarming situation is further exacerbated by the proliferation of computer games, another hazard of technological improvements. Staying at home in front of a computer screen can have a detrimental effect on a child's health and worryingly may contribute to the formation of personalities that are unaccustomed to the company of others. Again, rather than spending time collectively, whether with family or friends, as they would have once done, our young people are growing up in isolation, bereft of social interaction.

To what extent does blame for these problems lie in our failing to control the use of such technology, however, rather than in the technology itself? Whether we like it or not, technology is here to stay, and it cannot be denied that it has facilitated many obvious improvements in our abilities to interact with one another. Perhaps what we should be aiming for is sensible and restrained use rather than overindulgence or a complete ban. I would suggest that we are not in danger of losing our sense of 'society' through technological advancement; we are merely modifying our definition of what society means.

7 Memory games

It has been said that when working with young learners, introducing every learning activity as a game is a good way to increase motivation and make sure the learners participate with enthusiasm. With some adult classes the reverse may be true: that is, games may sometimes need to be presented as 'activities' for them to appreciate the potential for learning that they may contain.

This is an overgeneralization, of course, but what is true is that different learners, irrespective of their age, will respond differently to the idea of using games in the language classroom, and this needs to be considered when deciding on the way that any game is presented to a class.

From being a favourite pastime in Victorian drawing rooms to a way of easing the monotony of long car journeys in the era before Game Boy, the use of games that focus on memory has a long history. In the language class, they are a great way to provide repeated and intensive exposure to a particular area of language, as well as opportunities for retrieval. Another advantage of using memory games is that, though they may have a very explicit focus on language, the game is won or lost through the learners' ability to remember things, rather than on their ability to be accurate and correct in the language they are learning. This shift of emphasis is important in helping learners to avoid being embarrassed when they make mistakes. Some learners do have better memories than others, though, and in some of the activities there will be clear losers and winners. For this reason it is important to emphasize the light-hearted side of the game and to make sure that learners are competing in pairs or groups wherever possible so that any feelings of failure are kept to a minimum.

Name games

Teachers and learners are often faced with the mammoth task of learning by heart tens, sometimes hundreds, of names at the beginning of each term.

If everyone can quickly start using the names of the other participants in the class, however, it can be a step towards a more personalized and congenial learning environment. Here are six name games which can be used at the beginning of a group's life to facilitate this process.

- *Ball throwing*: A ball, or other soft object, is passed from one learner to another around the class. Learners say their own name in a loud and clear voice as they throw the ball to another person. Once everyone has had the ball at least once, the process is reversed, this time with learners having to remember the name of the person they are throwing the ball to. The class can be asked to do this as quickly as possible, or a second ball can also be introduced.
- *Names with adjectives*: Learner A says his or her name preceded by an adjective that begins with same sound (*I'm strong Xiaoli*, for example). Learner B does the same but also has to remember and repeat what Learner A said (*This is strong Xiaoli and I'm quiet Kamrun*). This process continues around the class with each new person who speaks having to repeat everything that was said before. If anyone has problems thinking of an adjective, the rest of the group help out. Adding gestures to go with the name and the adjective can also help to make things more memorable. Words other than adjectives can also be used (e.g. *swimming Xiaoli* or *King Kamrun*). See also the variation under Activity 7.3: *Language chains* on p. 191.
- *The history of my name*: Learners work in pairs. They tell each other about any meanings that their names may have, whether they were named after anyone, how they feel about their names, and about any nicknames that they have ever had. At the end everyone tells the rest of the class what they have found out about their partners.
- *Three times*: Learner A stands up. The learner's task is to say the name of another learner in the class (Learner B) three times, before Learner B can say Learner A's name once. If Learner A fails to do this, then he or she has another go. When Learner A does this successfully, Learner B becomes the one who has to stand up.
- *The blanket*: The class is divided into two groups and a blanket is held up between them. Each group secretly chooses one person to go up to the blanket. On the count of three, the blanket is dropped and the two selected people have to quickly say the name of the person they are facing. Whoever says it last has to join the other team.

- *Frankenstein*: Everyone stands in a big circle. Learner A says the name of another learner on the opposite side of the circle (Learner B). Learner A then walks *slowly* towards Learner B with arms outstretched (like Frankenstein!). Learner B now has to say quickly the name of a person on the other side from him or her (Learner C) and walk towards Learner C, before Learner A gets to him or her. Learner A then takes Learner B's place in the circle. If anyone gets to the person they have named before the other person speaks, that person loses.

7.1 Kim's game

Memory focus	Retrieving the names of a list of objects.
Level	Any
Time	10 minutes plus
Preparation	You will need a bag containing 8 to 15 objects. These could be food items or other household objects, etc.

Procedure

1 Open the bag and take out the objects one at a time, eliciting the name of each item as you do so. Talking about the objects with the learners (*Do you like this? Where do you keep yours?*, etc.) will help to make the items more memorable. Place the objects on the table in front of you where everyone can see them.

2 Allow some time for the learners to look at the objects and try to remember them all.

3 Quickly put the objects back into the bag so that they can no longer be seen.

4 Ask the learners to write down the names of all of the objects that they can remember.

5 Ask them to compare lists with a partner and to add anything they had forgotten. Which pair remembered the most objects?

6 Ask individual students to tell you the names of objects from their lists, producing the item from the bag again as they do so.

Follow-up

Ask each learner to take one of the objects/pictures and hide it under the desks in front of him or her. Try to remember which learner has which object and then ask questions to find out. This is a natural context in which to introduce *Do you have the X?* at beginner level, or expressions of modality such as *I'm pretty sure you're the one with the Y* at higher levels.

Variations

1 Using pictures rather than the objects themselves and using a data projector, if available, increases the range of language areas that can be practised (and puts less strain on the teacher's bag straps!). Images can be found using a picture search engine like Google Images™ (http://images.google.com/) and chosen because they relate to a particular lexical set such as clothing, forms of transport, etc. With pictures, learners can be asked to remember details as well as just the name (e.g. *A man wearing blue overalls, riding a bike*).

2 With the objects/pictures still on the table, ask the learners to close their eyes while you remove one of them. Can they tell you which item is missing when they look again?

7.2 What's different?

Memory focus	Remembering detail and talking about changes (this activity is a natural way of practising this use of the present perfect tense).
Level	Any
Time	5–10 minutes
Preparation	None

Procedure

1 Organize the class into pairs or small groups. Ask everyone to study each other's clothing carefully.

2 Now ask half the people from each pair or group to go out of the room briefly.

3 Those inside and out now change three things about their clothing (put their watches on the other wrist, undo their shoelaces, etc.).

4 Those who were outside now come back in again and everyone tells each other the differences that they notice.

Variation

While half the class is outside, those inside make 10 changes to the classroom itself (e.g. open the curtains, move the tables, etc.). When the learners come back in, they report on the changes they notice.

7.3 Language chains

Memory focus	Storing a learner-generated list of language items in working memory.
Level	Elementary and above
Time	5–10 minutes
Preparation	None

Procedure

1 Say this sentence to the class, using mime, gesture or translation to make meanings clear if necessary.

I went to the shop at the end of the road and I bought some apples.

2 Now choose somebody to continue the chain. This learner should repeat what you said and add something else.

I went to the shop at the end of the road and I bought some apples and a bicycle.

3 This learner now chooses another person to continue. Everything that has previously been said needs to be remembered and repeated each time, and something else needs to be added at the end. Language errors can be reformulated by the learners or the teacher as you go along.

4 When somebody makes a mistake by forgetting what somebody said, start a new chain. What is the longest chain of remembered language items that anyone can keep in their heads? You may wish to award a prize for the person who achieves this.

Follow-up

Ask the class to write down the longest sentence produced in the game.

Variations

1   This activity can be focused around particular areas of vocabulary such as lexical sets (food, sports equipment, etc.) containers (*a box of ...*, *a packet of ...*, etc.) or adjectives (learners use an adjective with each noun that they introduce).

2   Instead of focusing on vocabulary, this activity can also be used to practise an area of grammar. The first learner says a sentence using the target form.

I'm Hye Jun and I don't have a sister.

The next learner then repeats that sentence (changing the form if necessary) and adds another sentence about him- or herself, using the same form.

She's Hye Jun and she doesn't have a sister. I'm Severine and I don't smoke.

7.4 Remembering unusual sentences

Memory focus	Challenging learners to retrieve a large number of sentences using a particular structure.
Level	Elementary and above
Time	15 minutes plus
Preparation	None

Procedure

1   Decide on an area of language that needs practising and ask everyone to write down some sentences that relate to themselves using the form you have chosen (the past simple is focused on below). The sentences do not have to be true. In fact, writing something unusual will probably make the activity more interesting, and the sentences more memorable. Go round and check the learners' work for accuracy. For the past simple some examples could be:

I went to an underwater wedding reception at the weekend.

I built my own house out of cardboard boxes.

2   After a few minutes, ask everyone to get into pairs. Each pair now looks at all of their sentences and decides which of their sentences is the most interesting. This is now chosen as the one thing that they both did.

3 Each pair now mingles with the rest of the class. Each time they meet another pair of students, they should interact with them, telling each other the thing that they did, and asking a few questions to find out more information where possible. They should try to remember what everyone says to them.

4 When energy starts to drop, bring everyone back to their seats. Ask each pair of students to go through what all of the pairs that they met did.

5 Ask them to share this in feedback. The pair that remembers the most could be awarded a prize.

Variation
With classes of fewer than 15 people, students may work individually.

7.5 Slap, clap, click, click

Memory focus	Storing a bank of previously used language items in working memory, and making those language items memorable through rhythmic chanting.
Level	Any
Time	5 minutes plus
Preparation	None

Procedure

1 If you have the space, sit with the learners in a closed circle. If not, this activity can still be done with learners standing in their usual positions. Teach the class the following 1, 2, 3, 4 rhythm.
   1 Slap your thighs with both hands
   2 Clap
   3 Click the fingers on your left hand
   4 Click the fingers on your right hand

2 Decide in consultation with the learners on an area of vocabulary to review (for example, adjectives to describe people). Starting very slowly at first, show them how words can be chanted to fit in with the rhythm, by saying one word on the left click (e.g. *happy*) and a different word on the right (e.g. *friendly*). It is now the next person's turn to say a word.

If you are not working in a circle, you will need to agree on the order of the learners beforehand. The next person repeats the second word said by the person before (e.g. *friendly*) on the left click and then says a new word on the right click (e.g. *tired*).

3 Now do it with everyone doing the actions in time with each other. If someone makes a mistake by not keeping to the rhythm, or saying a word that has already been used or does not fit the category, you will have to start again. Try to beat the record for how many people can be involved in the chain before it breaks down.

Variations

1 This activity can also be used to review collocations with key words (*get, take, make, do, have*, etc.). The first person says a headword on the left click (e.g. *get*) and a word that collocates with it on the right click (e.g. *home*) on the second. The second person then repeats this with the first sequence (*get* on the first click and *home* on the second) and then does a different chunk for the second sequence (for example *get* on the first click and *married* on the second. This process continues with the third person, and so on.

2 Each learner chooses a different vocabulary item in the category and tells everybody what it is. The first person says their own item on the left click and then somebody else's on the right. The person whose item was said then has to continue the process.

3 Learner 1 says a word on the left click (*cat*) and a letter of the alphabet on the right click (*m*). Learner 2 says a word beginning with *m* (*mountain*) on the left click and a new letter on the right click (*d*). Learner 3 says a word beginning with *d* on the left click (*donkey*), etc. This can be made harder by restricting it to a large lexical set like food and drink.

7.6 Pelmanism

Memory focus	Challenging learners to hold a range of language items in working memory, and to recall the meanings of these items.
Level	Any
Time	10 minutes plus
Preparation	Each group of up to six learners needs a set of 20–40 cards of matching pairs. The matching pairs could consist of a word in L1 with a word in L2 (*tomorrow/mañana*), a word and a picture of the word (*a box of matches* / picture of a box of matches – see Box 7.6a), a word and its opposite meaning (*closed/open* – see Box 7.6b), or words that together form a strong collocation or fixed expression (see Box 7.6c).

Procedure

1 Each group of learners receives a set of the cards.
2 They spread them out on the table face down.
3 One learner in each group turns over two cards. If the two cards go together, he or she keeps them and takes another turn. If the cards do not go together, they are turned face down again and the turn passes to the next player.
4 As cards keep getting turned over, the learners start to remember where they are. The winner is the person with the most cards at the end.

Variation

As each card is turned over, learners have to say what is on the card that goes with it before trying to find that card. For instance, learners turn over a picture of a box of matches and have to say *a box of matches*. This happens whether they find matching pairs or not.

Follow-up

1 The cards are put away and the learners work in pairs to produce a list of all the language items used in the game that they can remember.
2 The learners go through the language items and come up with other words that collocate with the words being focused on. For instance, in Box 7.6b *curly* or *straight* hair is acceptable, but not a *curly* road.
3 Learners test each other by saying one part of the pair and asking the other learners in their group to recall the language item that goes with it.

Box 7.6a: Pelmanism

a box of matches	
a match	
a piece of cake	
a cake	
a bar of chocolate	
some chocolates	
a packet of crisps	
a handful of crisps	

continued

Box 7.6a: (*cont.*)

a tin of tuna	
a tuna	
a loaf of bread	
a slice of bread	
a jar of honey	
a spoonful of honey	
a carton of milk	
a glass of milk	

✂

From *Memory Activities for Language Learning*
© Cambridge University Press 2011

Box 7.6b: Pelmanism

The shops are **closed**.	The window's **open**.
This class is really **easy**.	The questions are quite **difficult**.
He's got **curly** hair.	It's a very **straight** road.
She's quite **short**.	It's a very **tall** building.
The food's **cheap**.	Everything's **expensive**.
The train was **early**.	She's **late** for work.
She's got **big** eyes.	His feet are quite **small**.
A **rich** businessman.	A **poor** person.
She's quite **thin**.	It's a **thick** book.
These grapes are **sour**.	This coffee's very **sweet**.
That's an **interesting** book.	The film was very **boring**.
The music's very **loud**.	She's very **quiet**.

✂

Box 7.6c: Pelmanism

I'm going out tonight. Will you be able …	… to **look after** the children?
Would you like to …	… **have a look round**?
We need to **look into** what's …	… been going on.
Why don't you **look it up** in the …	… dictionary?
Look …	… **out**!
She really **looks up** …	… **to him**.
She's really **looking forward to** meeting …	… you.
Things are **beginning to look up** a …	… bit.
No thanks, **I'm just** …	… **looking**.
It looks like it's going to …	… rain.

✂

From *Memory Activities for Language Learning*
© Cambridge University Press 2011   PHOTOCOPIABLE

7.7 Auditory Pelmanism

Memory focus	Training learners to hold and process language in working memory without visual clues.
Level	Any
Time	10 minutes plus
Preparation	Prepare a list of 10 matching pairs which have been randomly written next to the numbers 1 to 20. See Box 7.7a for an example. A set of cards with the numbers from 1 to 20 are then stuck to a wall or whiteboard in the classroom.

Procedure

1 Organize the class into no more than four teams.
2 Each team chooses two of the numbers on the board. For each number read out the corresponding language item. For example:

Team A: Number ten.
Teacher: Russia.
Team A: Number 19.
Teacher: What's the fastest land animal?

If the two sentences go together, the corresponding numbers are taken down from the board and given to the team. They then have another go. If the two sentences do not go together, the turn passes to the next team.
3 As with standard Pelmanism (see Activity 7.6), the winners are the team that ends up with the most cards.

Follow-up

Learners work together to produce a written list of all of the language items that were used in the game that they can remember.

Variations

1 This activity can also be done in small groups. Each group spreads a set of the numbered cards out on the table. One learner has the sheet of paper with the matching pairs written on it (kept hidden from the rest of the group) and takes the role of the teacher in the procedure outlined above. The others spread out the set of 20 cards on the table. They play the game by taking it in turns to choose numbers and these are read out by the learner with the sheet.

For homework learners prepare a sheet like the one in Box 7.7a to focus on an area of language assigned by the teacher. These can then be used to play the game in small groups in the next class. Teams take it in turns to choose two numbers and the learner who prepared the sheet reads out the two corresponding sentences.

2   Instead of simply saying the utterances, other formats are also possible. For instance, one half of the numbers are the names of animals and the other half are the sounds that the animals make. Or one half describe situations and the other half are mimed versions of the situations. See Box 7.7b for a sheet using this principle which focuses on the language of aches and pains.

Box 7.7a: Auditory Pelmanism

1   Where is the highest waterfall in the world?
2   The cheetah.
3   The Vatican City.
4   What's the highest mountain in the world?
5   China.
6   What's the longest river in the world?
7   Which is the biggest country in the world?
8   Everest.
9   What's the largest bird in the world?
10 Russia.
11 Which city has the largest population?
12 In Venezuela.
13 The ostrich.
14 Which country has the largest population?
15 Tokyo.
16 What's the biggest animal in the world?
17 The blue whale.
18 What's the smallest country in the world?
19 What's the fastest land animal?
20 The Nile.

From *Memory Activities for Language Learning*
© Cambridge University Press 2011   PHOTOCOPIABLE

Box 7.7b: Auditory Pelmanism

1   Say: I've got a thorn in my finger.
2   Say: My legs are a bit stiff.
3   Mime: My hands are freezing.
4   Say: I've got a splitting headache.
5   Mime: I've got a nosebleed.
6   Mime: I've got a thorn in my finger.
7   Mime: My back's killing me.
8   Say: I've got a dodgy stomach.
9   Mime: My legs are a bit stiff.
10 Say: I've got really bad toothache.
11 Say: I've got a pain in my neck.
12 Mime: I've got a splitting headache.
13 Mime: I've got a dodgy stomach.
14 Say: My head itches like mad.
15 Say: I've got a nosebleed.
16 Say: My back's killing me.
17 Say: My hands are freezing.
18 Mime: My head itches like mad.
19 Mime: I've got really bad toothache.
20 Mime: I've got a pain in my neck.

7.8 First-letter hints

Memory focus	Holding a range of idiomatic expressions in working memory and challenging retrieval of them.
Level	Upper intermediate and above
Time	10 minutes plus
Preparation	Each group of learners needs a set of cards (see Box 7.8a) and an answer sheet (see Box 7.8b).

Procedure

1 Divide the class up into small groups of at least three and give each group a set of cards. They spread them out face down on the table.

2 One learner in each group is given the answer sheet with the complete expressions and their meanings. This person acts as a judge and does not take part in the game.

3 The other learners take it in turns to turn over a card. If they think they can complete the set expression, they check with the judge and, if correct, they keep the piece of paper. The judge then makes sure that everyone understands the expression. If a learner cannot complete the expression correctly, he or she places it face down again where it was. Play then passes to the next player (whether they completed the expression or not).

4 As more and more cards are turned over, learners start to remember how to complete the expressions. The winner is the person with the most cards at the end.

Follow-up

Learners go through all the cards again, personalizing the expressions by using them to talk about themselves or people they know. Ask learners to prepare their own cards for homework using a site like http://idioms.thefreedictionary.com/

Note

The idea for this activity comes from *Teaching Chunks of Language: From Noticing to Remembering* by Seth Lindstomberg and Frank Boers, London: Heibling Languages, 2008.

Box 7.8a: First-letter hints

That must've cost a pretty p …	That must've cost a p … penny.
I need to p … up the courage to tell her.	I need to pluck up the c … to tell her.
To add i … to injury she took all my stuff as well.	To add insult to i … she took all my stuff as well.
She's a woman after my own h … .	She's a woman a … my own heart.
It's just a s … throw from where I live.	It's just a stone's t … from where I live.
He's the s … image of his dad.	He's the spitting i … of his dad.
In the l … run I think things will be OK.	In the long r … I think things will be OK.
I've got a b … to pick with you.	I've got a bone to p … with you.
You're your own worst e … .	You're your own w … enemy.
His h … is in the right place.	His heart is in the right p … .

✂

Box 7.8b: First-letter hints

That must've cost a pretty penny. (That must've cost a lot of money.)

You're your own worst enemy. (You are the cause of your own problems.)

I need to pluck up the courage to tell her. (I need to make myself feel brave so that I can tell her.)

To add insult to injury she took all my stuff as well. (As well as all the other bad things she did, she took all my stuff.)

It's just a stone's throw from where I live. (It's very close to where I live.)

He's the spitting image of his dad. (He looks just like his dad.)

I've got a bone to pick with you. (I'm annoyed with you and I need to talk to you about it.)

In the long run I think things will be OK. (Eventually I think things will be OK.)

She's a woman after my own heart. (She likes the same things or behaves in the same way as I do.)

His heart is in the right place. (He's really a kind person who is doing his best to do the right thing.)

From *Memory Activities for Language Learning*

7.9 The collocation game

Memory focus	Recognizing common collocations.
Level	Elementary and above
Time	10 minutes plus
Preparation	Each group of four or five learners will need a set of headwords and collocate cards. The example in Box 7.9 is for an elementary/pre-intermediate group. The headwords and collocate cards work best printed onto thick paper or card so that learners cannot see through them.

Procedure

1 Divide the learners into groups of four or five. Give each group a set of the cards, and ask them to work together and match each headword with its seven collocates.

2 Go through the answers together, checking that everyone has got them right.

3 The collocate cards are now turned face down, mixed up and spread randomly on the table. Each person takes one of the headwords. (There will be one left over if there are only four people in the group.) They now take turns to turn over a collocate card. If it fits with their headword, they keep it and have another go. If it does not fit, they replace it face down again, and it is the next person's go. The person who finds all of his or her collocates first is the winner.

Follow-up

1 If groups finish quickly the learners can swap headwords and play the game again.

2 They test each other on the collocates which go with each person's headword.

3 They write personalized sentences using some of the collocations.

Box 7.9: The collocation game

HAVE	a shower	a party	an argument
a good time	a problem	an accident	a headache
GO	fishing	swimming	out
for a walk	to a party	on holiday	home
PLAY	chess	cards	the guitar
computer games	an instrument	tennis	football
DO	some cooking	your homework	karate
some cleaning	the dishes	some exercise	business
MAKE	friends with someone	a decision	an appointment
your bed	a lot of noise	a mess	a mistake

From *Memory Activities for Language Learning*
© Cambridge University Press 2011   PHOTOCOPIABLE

7.10 The suffix game

Memory focus	Making a list of common abstract nouns memorable through challenging repeated retrieval.
Level	Upper intermediate and above
Time	10 minutes plus
Preparation	Each group of two to four learners will need a complete set of the word cards in Box 7.10 (cut up into individual slips) and a maximum of eight coins or counters.

Procedure

1 Establish with the class how abstract nouns are often formed by adding a suffix to the end of other word forms. Give a few examples on the board if necessary. For example:

confident + -ence = confidence

frequent + -cy = frequency

treat + -ment = treatment

2 Organize the class into groups of two to four. Give each group a set of the word and suffix cards in Box 7.10.

3 Ask them to work as a group to match each suffix (the words in capitals) to two other words to form abstract nouns.

4 Deal with any difficulties as you go round the groups, or with the whole class together at the end.

Answers: breakage, wastage, proposal, refusal, robbery, bribery, development, employment, expansion, inclusion, acceptance, attendance, demonstration, alteration, dependence, interference, responsibility, similarity, friendship, hardship, consciousness, darkness

5 Now ask each group to put the 22 word cards face up in a circle formation on the table in front of them (see the picture of the game set-up on p. 209). They should be placed in a random order. The suffix cards are now mixed up and placed face down (randomly again) inside the circle. (The picture shows one suffix card turned over to illustrate Procedure 6b on p. 209.) Each player places two coins or counters, one on top of the other, on one of the 22 word cards, and as far away as possible from the other players' coins.

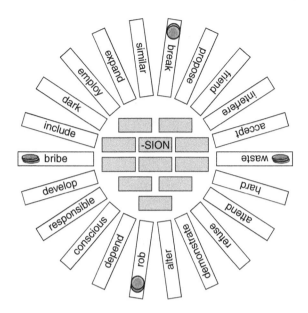

6 This game is far easier to demonstrate than to explain. If possible ask everyone to gather round one group's table in order to do this. The rules of the game are as follows:

  a) Players take it in turns to try to move round the circle in a clockwise direction. They do this by finding the suffix card which goes with the word card which is next in the sequence.

  b) If they turn over one of the suffix cards in the middle and it goes with the next card in the sequence, they move their two coins forward and have another turn. If not, they remain where they are and play passes to the next person. In the beginning it is only by luck that someone will be able to move forward, but gradually, as more and more cards get turned over, people start to remember where the cards that they need are located.

  c) When a player lands on a card immediately behind another player's coins they have the chance to steal the top coin from that player. They can do this by finding the suffix card which goes with the word card immediately after the other player's coins. If they manage to do this, they jump over that player and steal any top coins that he or she may have.

  d) The object of the game is to steal the top coins of all the other players. The person who does this is the winner.

Box 7.10: The suffix game

-AGE	break	waste
-AL	propose	refuse
-ERY	rob	bribe
-MENT	develop	employ
-SION	expand	include
-ANCE	accept	attend
-TION	demonstrate	alter
-ENCE	depend	interfere
-ITY	responsible	similar
-SHIP	friend	hard
-NESS	conscious	dark

✂

From *Memory Activities for Language Learning*
© Cambridge University Press 2011   PHOTOCOPIABLE

Note
Depending on class size, it may be more appropriate for players to play in pairs within their groups. This way there can be more than four people in each group.

References and further reading

Alloway, T. (2010) *Improving Working Memory*. London: Sage

Baddeley, A. (2004) *Your Memory: A User's Guide*. London: Carlton Books

Bolinger, D. (1961) Syntactic blends and other matters, *Language*, 37: 366–81

Bryant, D. (1990) Implicit associative responses influence encoding in memory, *Memory and Cognition*, 18(4): 348–58

Buzan, T. (1993) *The Mind Map Book*. London: BBC Books

Chomsky, N. (1959) Review of Verbal Behavior by B. F. Skinner, *Language*, 35: 26–57

Cook, G. (2000) *Language Play, Language Learning*. Oxford: Oxford University Press

Council of Europe (2001) *A Common European Framework of Reference for Languages: Learning, Teaching, Assessment*. Cambridge: Cambridge University Press

Curran, C. (1972) *Counseling-Learning: A Whole-Person Model for Education*. New York: Grune and Stratton

Davis, P. and Rinvolucri, M. (1988) *Dictation: New Methods, New Possibilities*. Cambridge: Cambridge University Press

Davis, P. and Rinvolucri, M. (1995) *More Grammar Games*. Cambridge: Cambridge University Press

Ding, Y. (2007) Text memorisation and imitation: the practices of successful Chinese learners of English, *System*, 35: 271–80

Doff, A. and Jones, C. (1994) *Language in Use: Intermediate, Student's Book 1*. Cambridge: Cambridge University Press

Dolby, K. (2009) *Mrs Dolby's Memory Magic*. London: Random House

Ellis, N. C. (2001) Memory for language, in P. Robinson, ed., *Cognition and Second Language Instruction*. Cambridge: Cambridge University Press (pp. 33–68)

Heath, C. and Heath, D. (2008) *Made to Stick: Why Some Ideas Take Hold and Others Come Unstuck*. London: Arrow Books

Heathfield, D. (2005) *Spontaneous Speaking: Drama Activities for Confidence and Fluency*. Peaslake: Delta Publishing

Higbee, K. (2001) *Your Memory: How It Works and How to Improve It*. Philadelphia: Avalon Group

Hopper, P. (1998) Emergent grammar, in M. Tomasello, ed., *The New Psychology of Language*. Mahwah, NJ: Lawrence Erlbaum Associates (pp. 155–75)

Houston, H. (2009) *Provoking Thought. Memory and Thinking in ELT*. Lexington, KY: Anthimeria Press

Keddie, J. (2009) *Images*. Oxford: Oxford University Press

Lewis, M. (1993) *The Lexical Approach: The State of ELT and a Way Forward*. Hove: Language Teaching Publications

Lewis, M. (1997) *Implementing the Lexical Approach: Putting Theory into Practice*. Hove: Language Teaching Publications

Lindstromberg, S. and Boers, F. (2008) *Teaching Chunks of Language: From Noticing to Remembering*. London: Heibling Languages

Mumford, S. (2008) Making grammar memorable, *Humanising Language Teaching*, December 2008 (available online at http://www.hltmag.co.uk/dec08/mart03.htm)

Nation, I. (2001) *Learning Vocabulary in Another Language*. Cambridge: Cambridge University Press

Noice, H. and Noice, T. (2006) What studies of actors and acting can tell us about memory and cognitive functioning, *Current Directions in Psychological Science*, 15 (1): 14–18 (available online at http://www.psychologicalscience.org/pdf/cd/actors_memory.pdf)

Parkinson, J. (2007) *I Before E (Except after C: Old-School Ways to Remember Stuff*. London: Michael O'Mara Books

Puchta, H. and Stranks, J. (2010) *English in Mind Student's Book 1*, Second edition. Cambridge: Cambridge University Press

Scheller, I. (2004) *Szenische Interpretation*. Seelze-Velber: Kallmeyersche Verlagsbuchhandlung

Singleton, D. (1999) *Exploring the Second Language Mental Lexicon*. Cambridge: Cambridge University Press

Skehan, P. (1998) *A Cognitive Approach to Language Learning*. Oxford: Oxford University Press

Stevick, E. (1980) *Teaching Languages: A Way and Ways*. Boston, MA: Heinle and Heinle

Stevick, E. (1996) *Memory, Meaning and Method: A View of Language Teaching*, Second edition. Boston, MA: Heinle and Heinle

Stevick, E (1998) *Working with Teaching Methods: What's at Stake?* Boston, MA: Heinle ELT

Sweet, H. (1899) *The Practical Study of Language: A Guide for Teachers and Learners*. London: J. M. Dent & Co.

Taggart, C. (2008) *I Used to Know That: Stuff You Forgot from School*. London: Michael O'Mara Books

Thornbury, S. (2004) *Natural Grammar: The Keywords of English and How They Work*. Oxford: Oxford University Press

Willis, D. (2003) *Rules, Patterns and Words: Grammar and Lexis in English Language Teaching*. Cambridge: Cambridge University Press

Wray, A. (2008) *Formulaic Language: Pushing the Boundaries*. Oxford: Oxford University Press

Wright, A. (1987) *How to Improve Your Mind*. Cambridge: Cambridge University Press

Websites

The following websites contain useful resources and activities related to the role of memory in language learning.

http://forbetterenglish.com/
Search for common collocations and other chunks of language by typing a key word in English into a box.

http://puzzlemaker.discoveryeducation.com/
Easily create word searches, crosswords and other types of puzzle for language retrieval exercises.

http://www.script-o-rama.com/
http://www.songlyrics.com/
http://web.orange.co.uk/p/news/quirkies
http://www.youtube.com/
Find extracts from film scripts, song lyrics or short news stories for learning by heart.

http://www.rhymezone.com/
Look for words in a rhyming dictionary.

http://www.memorizenow.com/
Paste or type short texts, poems or song lyrics into a box. The text can then automatically be converted into a range of different memory exercises involving flash cards, first-letter hints or lines representing words.

http://www.2flashgames.com/learning_english_games.htm
A bank of simple online memory games for vocabulary development.

http://tracyalloway.com/
Access resources and articles related to the role of working memory in education by the psychologist Tracey Alloway.

http://www.memory-key.com/
Read articles and reports on the role of memory in education.

http://quizlet.com/
Use or create online word cards.

Index

Dialogue Activities

Exploring spoken interaction in the language class

Nick Bilbrough

Do your students wonder why the language they cover in class is often different from the spoken language they encounter outside the classroom?

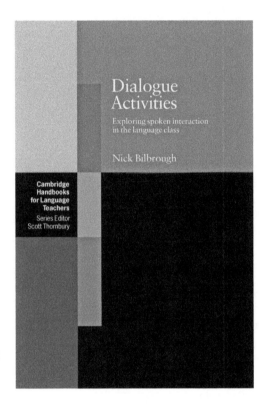

This book provides practical ideas to encourage students to look at spoken language in different contexts through the use of transcripts and authentic conversations. It will help them to identify what features of language are used in spoken language and how to sound more natural when they speak themselves.

By adopting a view of dialogue as being both 'product' and 'process', *Dialogue Activities* covers a broad range of teaching purposes including:

- the use of written and recorded coursebook dialogues

- the use of dialogue extracts from literature

- the use of authentic conversation extracts

- the scripting and performance of original dialogues by learners

- the use of dialogue as a means of communicating personal meaning

- the use of teacher-learner dialogue as a means of contextualizing learning

- the history of dialogue use in language teaching

- criteria for dialogue choice and design.

The book also includes a bank of dialogues which can be used with the activities or used by teachers as models for their own materials.

'*A fantastic resource.*' QATESOL NEWSLETTER

Paperback 978 0 521 68951 9

Psychology for Language Teachers

A social constructivist approach

Marion Williams and Robert L. Burden

This important book brings together some of the most recent developments and thinking in the field of educational psychology with issues of concern to many language teachers. It considers various ways in which a deeper understanding of the discipline of educational psychology can help language teachers. The first part of the book presents an overview of educational psychology and discusses how different approaches to psychology have influenced language-teaching methodology. Following this, four themes are identified: the learner, the teacher, the task and the learning context. Recent psychological developments in each of these domains are discussed and implications are drawn for language teaching.

Psychology for Language Teachers will be of central interest to every teacher concerned with issues such as approaches to learning, motivation, the role of the individual, attribution, mediation, the teaching of thinking, the cognitive demands of tasks and the learning environment.

The book does not assume any previous knowledge of psychology.

Paperback 978 0 521 49880 7

Personalizing Language Learning

Griff Griffiths and Kathy Keohane

Would you like to use materials that are personally relevant to your learners?

Personalizing Language Learning provides guidance and practical activities for teachers who are looking for ways to make language learning more person-centred. Taking the learner as the starting point, the book presents a range of ready-to-use materials which draw on the personal experiences, thoughts, feelings and opinions of the learner.

These user-friendly materials will appeal to all teachers looking for materials with engaging and meaningful content.

Paperback 978 0 521 63364 2

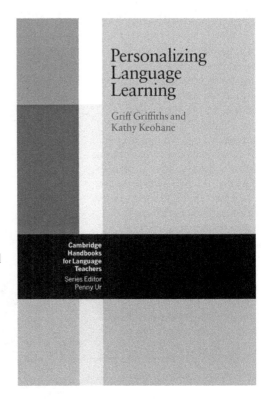

Personalizing Language Learning

Griff Griffiths and Kathy Keohane

Cambridge Handbooks for Language Teachers
Series Editor Penny Ur